What people are saying

T0016212

The Christ and Jesus: The Difference

With remarkable clarity, Don MacGregor reveals to us the important distinction between the Christ and the historical Jesus. Though traditionally considered to be the same individual, he untangles the two to show that the life of Jesus set the note for the Christian Tradition, whilst evidence of the Christ and the Christ Principle can be found within several religious faiths. This book beautifully highlights how the Perennial Philosophy is foundational to many of the mystical truths of Christianity, and also includes a rich and insightful exploration into the subject of reincarnation, together with the biblical verses that are suggestive of its existence.

William Meader, international speaker and author of *Shine Forth: The Soul's Magical Destiny,* Portland, Oregon, USA

In this third book in Don MacGregor's Wisdom Series, the author continues to set out his convictions that our world is diffused with the perennial wisdom common to all religions, whereby the all-pervasive divine energy can be realised as the highest form of consciousness, as seen in Jesus. In this understanding Jesus was one with the cosmic, universal Christ, revealing that divine principle through which the reality of God is seen in our world. MacGregor reinterprets the events of Jesus' life from birth to death and resurrection as the journey of soul making, upon which all humans are engaged. Alongside chapters on the mystical Christ and Christ and other faiths, there is also a strong and convincing argument for reincarnation. Overall the book and the series show not only a wealth of reading and argument but a conviction stemming from the author's personal experiences which he is unafraid to detail. A valuable contribution to a progressive Christian faith.

Revd Canon Adrian Alker, Chair, Progressive Christian Network Britain

Open-hearted and open-minded, Don MacGregor's latest book is an insightful and intelligent exploration of the true nature of Jesus and his relationship with God. The book's approach is multi-faith in the very best way. It is also courageous as the author is an Anglican priest and dares openly to explore how Jesus can be understood through the perspective of reincarnation and the mystical teachings of other traditions. Highly recommended for anyone seeking a wider and deeper appreciation of Jesus and Christian teachings.

William Bloom, educator and author, director of the Spiritual Companions Trust

What could be more significant than freeing Jesus of Nazareth from the prison of confining belief created for him by the political and institutional powers of our world? In a well-researched and informative way, Don MacGregor does precisely this in the latest book in his Wisdom Series. What's more, *The Christ and Jesus* is filled with the warmth of Don's own life story. The reader is left to feel greater spiritual intimacy with the Christ Spirit and a greater love and appreciation for a man who brought it so vividly to the world.

David Karchere, Spiritual Director of the Emissaries of Divine Light, author of *Becoming a Sun: Emotional and Spiritual Intelligence for a Happy, Fulfilling Life*

This work is the fruit of years of deep theological reflection (and personal struggle), yet MacGregor's clear, accessible style wears the results of scholarship and life experience lightly. It could easily be read in an afternoon: absorbing and understanding its contents could change the course of a lifetime. The book serves two audiences particularly well. For Christians whose minds and hearts are awakening to a broader horizon than the conventional Christological doctrines, it opens a window into wisdom teachings on this subject that have remained to some extent hidden throughout history. These teachings, sometimes called the Perennial Philosophy or the Ageless Wisdom, are in accord with the experiences of the great mystics of all faiths. It is also an excellent primer for students of the Ageless Wisdom who wish to deepen their understanding of the connection between the Christ as an eternal spiritual fact and his historical manifestation in the person of Jesus of Nazareth, and to learn more about the evolution of this idea within Christian doctrine. **Dominic Dibble**, World Goodwill/Lucis Trust

The acid test of any book is not whether the reader agrees with it, but whether it causes him or her to reflect on new questions they had not examined before. Don MacGregor has certainly produced such a book. This is the third in a series that "seeks to reach those followers of the teachings of Jesus who are open to a wider theology and philosophy than that of traditional Church teaching." Conventional Christians might find it disturbing, but those who are prepared to look outside the box of traditional theology will be stimulated. He starts from a theological debate many have written about, what exactly is the relationship between the Jesus of History and the Christ of Faith? But the new perspective he brings arises from his interest in what he calls the "Perennial or Ageless Wisdom Philosophy, which traces an underlying stream of teaching which is primarily about inner transformation of the human being." I much commend this thought-provoking book.
The Revd Dr Robert Reiss, Canon Emeritus of Westminster, author of *Death, Where Is Your Sting*

In *The Christ and Jesus*, Don MacGregor calls on a lifetime's study of universal wisdom teachings and profound personal insights to clearly and significantly differentiate between Jesus as a human being and the Christ as the full embodiment of soul-level divinity. Discerning such Christ consciousness as the highest expression of unitive awareness that we as humans can experience and embody, the book offers a powerfully compelling perception of an evolutionary journey in terms of a soul's reincarnations through human lifetimes. Showing Jesus as an exemplar of the Christed potential that each of us has, it calls and inspires us to live and love our soul's fulfilled destiny. **Dr Jude Currivan,** Cosmologist, author of *The Cosmic Hologram* and forthcoming book *Gaia: Her-Story,* and co-founder of WholeWorld-View: www.wholeworld-view.org

Concluding this short, inspiring book, Don MacGregor writes: "It is my belief that in order to survive in the twenty-first century as a credible belief, Christianity has to take on board some of the precepts and understandings of the Ageless Wisdom teachings, especially as the leading edge of science is now putting forward the idea that there is a universal consciousness from which everything stems at a deep level of reality." Drawing on insights from the Ageless Wisdom texts as well as his own scientific and theological background, Don MacGregor weaves a new Christian narrative beyond the narrow denominational constructs of the past to a liberating and empowering vision of Jesus as the Christ. This "multilevel Christ" represents that ancient oneness known to mystics across the ages. This valuable synthesis of complex ideas is written in a lucid style, proving a timely resource for spiritual seekers in the twenty-first century. **Fr. Diarmuid O'Murchu,** social psychologist and R.C. priest, author of *Quantum Theology* and many other titles.

The Christ and Jesus: The Difference takes the reader on a roller-coaster journey exploring exciting and complex beliefs and concepts surrounding the historical Jesus, the Cosmic and Universal Christ, and Christ consciousness. It invites each one of us to consider where we fit into a constantly evolving and compassionate universe. Profoundly thought-provoking beliefs concerning reincarnation, the law of karma and the office of the Maitreya Christ will invite lively discussion and debate. Don MacGregor encourages us to take another look at the message of empowerment and transformation Jesus brought to our world. **Pam Evans MBE,** Founder of the multi award winning Peace Mala educational charity for global citizenship and world peace, and author of *Sharing the Light: Walking for World Peace with the Celtic Saints of Gower* and *How the Wisdom of the Ages Is Reflected in Many World Religions*

In this book, Don MacGregor guides us in an exploration into what or who is the Christ. He suggests that the Christ is a state of being that Jesus fully embodied, which can be realised by everyone, including ourselves, who is similarly spiritually evolved. Don draws on Christian teaching and that of other faiths, observations of the natural world and Wisdom teachings related to the Christian tradition. He uses his own journey of spiritual discovery in an open, modest and engaging way to illustrate this material. He encourages us to consider the idea of reincarnation, present in many spiritual traditions and sometimes in Christianity, as one way to understand how it might be possible for you and me to realise the state of Christhood. This is a short book with a large vision which challenges us to dip beneath the surface into the heart of Christian practice. **Jo Parsons**, Co-Director, the School of Christian Mysticism

Don MacGregor skilfully uses his own experiences of his journey to present and demonstrate a reflective encounter with the teachings of Christianity and specifically the differences between Jesus, and the Christ. He takes care to consider this difference in a new and inclusive way. The reader is invited to regard Jesus as a worthy role model. The *Christ consciousness* that Jesus achieved is an evolving compassionate consciousness that brings *love and wisdom* to life as a daily reverential encounter with relationships inner and outer, near, and far and with all that is. This Christ Consciousness is an inherent aspect of *divinity* within everyone and is awaiting its own germination into a more light-filled understanding.

Janet Derwent, Sundial House Group for Creative Meditation

The Christ and Jesus: The Difference

THE WISDOM SERIES BOOK 3

The Christ and Jesus: The Difference

The Wisdom Series Book 3

Don MacGregor

CHRISTIAN ALTERNATIVE
BOOKS

Winchester, UK
Washington, USA

JOHN HUNT PUBLISHING

First published by Christian Alternative Books, 2023
Christian Alternative Books is an imprint of John Hunt Publishing Ltd.,
No. 3 East St., Alresford, Hampshire SO24 9EE, UK
office@jhpbooks.com
www.johnhuntpublishing.com
www.christian-alternative.com

For distributor details and how to order please visit the 'Ordering' section on our website.

Text copyright: Don MacGregor 2021

ISBN: 978 1 80341 136 1
978 1 80341 137 8 (ebook)
Library of Congress Control Number: 2021952243

Design: Stuart Davies

UK: Printed and bound by CPI Group (UK) Ltd, Croydon, CR0 4YY
US: Printed and bound by Thomson-Shore, 7300 West Joy Road, Dexter, MI 48130

We operate a distinctive and ethical publishing philosophy in all areas of our business, from our global network of authors to production and worldwide distribution.

Contents

Previous Titles by the author

Christianity Expanding: Into Universal Spirituality. The Wisdom Series Book 1. Christian Alternative Books, John Hunt Publishing, 2020
ISBN 978-1-78904-422-5

Expanding Scriptures: Lost and Found. The Wisdom Series Book 2. Christian Alternative Books, John Hunt Publishing, 2022
ISBN 978-1-78904-866- 7

Blue Sky God: The Evolution of Science and Christianity. Circle Books, John Hunt Publishing, 2012
ISBN 978-1-84694-937-1

Introduction to the Wisdom Series

This book is the third in the Wisdom Series. The whole series seeks to reach those followers of the teachings of Jesus who are open to a wider theology and philosophy than that of traditional Church teaching. Hence it may not be for those who are quite content with the teaching, rituals and theology which they receive in the institutional Church. It draws on the Perennial or Ageless Wisdom Philosophy, which traces an underlying stream of teaching which is primarily about inner transformation of the human being. The teachings have been clothed in various systems of religion, from the ancient mystery schools of Egypt and Greece and early Hindu and Chinese philosophies, to all the major faiths of today. Each has expressed a part of it, which has often become ritualised and crystallised in form as time has passed. Today, we find it coming much more to the surface, as both modern spiritual teachings and the leading edge of scientific exploration into consciousness are both expressing something of this ancient wisdom.

Christianity has become crystallised in its institutional form, and in my small opinion needs to break free from such constriction. Jesus the Christ taught a path of transformation into deeper compassionate being. His call was to love one another, even to love our enemy. It was a call to oneness of being with all creation. Traditional Church theology in its simple form has turned it into a transaction between God and humanity, via the death of Jesus, to gain a place in heaven. In its earliest days, it was much more about transformation to a better way of being, rising above the lower nature, the "flesh". This is the essential teaching of the Perennial Wisdom, that we have a lower nature, the Personality, and a higher nature, the Soul. The Personality is self-centred in its emotions and thoughts, and needs to be infused with, and submit to, the loving compassionate Christ-consciousness of the soul. My vision is that expanding into this Wisdom philosophy can restore that central aspect of transformation to the core of Christianity, and also provide a framework for belief in the twenty-first century.

In addition to Christian theology, my own path brought me to the teachings of Theosophy and then the writings of Alice A. Bailey, in communication with a personage called the Tibetan, by the name of Djwhal Khul. Alice Bailey started off as an Anglican, married to a priest, so her take on the teaching is influenced by Christian terminology. These teachings go into great detail in twenty-four books, describing a vast interconnected cosmology of spiritual energies, planes and beings which make up the coherent whole. This whole is the One Life, the Source, the Godhead which permeates and is at the heart of everything. Her books are a mixture of psychology, philosophy, spirituality and soul astrology (very different from the frothy stuff in popular culture). It is my path to go deeper into this teaching, but also to provide an introduction to it as a viable expansion of Christianity for the future. The previous books in the series are:

Book One: *Christianity Expanding: Into Universal Spirituality.* This sets the scene for the whole series, setting out various areas of exploration that Christianity is moving into. From the global shift in consciousness to the need for change within Christianity, it introduces the evolving scientific world-view and the ecological imperatives that are upon us. It also highlights some of the theological issues that are tackled in further books in the series.

Book Two: *Expanding Scriptures: Lost and Found.* This looks into the lost but now rediscovered texts from the early church, the texts that were proscribed by the "winners" in the development of theology, largely as a result of Christianity

2

being adopted as the official religion of the Roman Empire. Many of these texts present the idea of *transformation* rather than *transaction*, representing the "lost Christianity". It dives into the Gospel of Thomas and also delves into the role of Mary Magdalene as the one who best understood Jesus. The tricky issue of language and translations is tackled, and it finally looks at the fascinating symbolism of numerology in the New Testament.

In this, **Book Three**, I dive into the tricky topic of how the human Jesus differs from the Universal Christ. There are three more books planned in the series, and the next one will look at the science of spirituality, touching in on quantum consciousness, epigenetics, biocentrism, pansychism, panspiritism, morphic resonance and many other theories which link in with the Perennial Philosophy teachings and an expanded view of Christianity. I aim to simplify and clarify the science to make clear the overlap with spiritual teachings. For thirteen years, I taught science to the 11–16 age range, so I hope to put that experience to good use!

The Wisdom Teachings

The whole Wisdom cosmology encompasses and speaks into everything that happens in the physical realm and particularly all areas of human endeavour – religion, economics, politics, education, health, relationships, psychology, etc. To get into the detail is something beyond this book, but to give an idea of its purpose, it seeks to encourage the following themes:

- **Right Human Relationships** – Foundational to the Wisdom teachings is the need for loving understanding and compassion, non-judgementalism, and acceptance of the inherent dignity of every human being. It is a commitment to finding wise outcomes in all relationships.

- **Goodwill**, which is a powerful principle, an attitude of being towards all other beings, human and non-human, wanting the best for them. It is a quality that generates kindness and warmth. It is the will-to-good.
- **Unanimity**, which is a form of group consciousness, appreciating the need to work together positively for a better world. It puts agreement and union of the Whole above the individual. The consensus so achieved is inclusive and transformative.
- **Group Endeavour** – seeking cooperation and collaboration rather than competition and antagonism. It is working together creatively such that use is made of mutual qualities. The ability to work with a common team purpose demonstrates the co-operation and interdependence of all.
- **Spiritual Approach** is the gradual path of transformation. It begins when we start to turn our attention from the material world around us and begin searching for a relationship with our inner true essence, our Higher Self, our Soul. Personal wisdom is acquired daily through all relationships and experiences when they are viewed in the light of the Soul.
- **Essential Divinity** is the recognition of the vital essence at our very core, the oneness that colours all our relationships revealing that we are all different and yet all the same, coming from the One Life, the Divine Source.

Within this open and expansive philosophical framework, Christianity and most other faiths can be expressed. Every religious tradition has its own scriptures which it holds to dearly, yet this wisdom stream runs through all of them, expressed in the culture and context of the particular faith. In this rapidly changing world, a larger container is urgently needed to overcome the seeming disparities and enmities between the different religious factions, and to encompass the huge rise of alternative and complementary spiritual, psychological and therapeutic practices which have emerged in recent years. The Perennial Wisdom teachings are enormous in their remit and give a presentation of a spiritual cosmology and psychology which is based in the existence of subtle energy realms and different spiritual planes constituting the makeup of the human being and all material reality.

In a simple analogy, it can be likened to a car which takes you from A to B safely. The purpose of the car is for transport to a different place. Most do not need to know the workings of the engine and its science, only that we can rely upon them. Some do need to look into the engineering, the chemistry and physics and subtle details of how a car works. Like a car, the wisdom philosophy has a whole host of levels of understanding from which to access it and understand it, but not everyone needs to be a mechanic or an electrical engineer or a research scientist. Just driving the car from A to B is enough. Transportation can become transformation if the themes of the Wisdom teachings are followed, which can happen via any enlightened spiritual path, and particularly within the teachings and example of Jesus the Christ.

Chapter 1

The Christ and Jesus – the Hardest Question

This book raises one of the hardest topics for any Christian who is opening up to a wider and deeper faith. Are the Christ and Jesus the same or different? The answer is an ambiguously definite yes and no! In exploring this topic, I introduce the concept of reincarnation from the Wisdom teachings in order to make greater sense of some Christian theology from my point of view. This is a big step for a traditional Christian to take, as it means many central Church teachings have to be re-worked as well as much of the hymnody and liturgy. It has taken many years to piece this all together in my spiritual understanding, and it has been a time of doubt and faith, with feelings of guilt at moving on, yet rejoicing in a belief that makes more sense to me in the world today. I hope it may help others who are on a similar path.

A Different Viewpoint

I didn't start going to church as an adult until I was thirty years old. I was a science teacher at the time, teaching 11–16-year-olds general science and physics. During my time of teaching, I had become interested in the bigger questions of life, and got involved in the early ecological movement, questioning what we are here for, what life is about and so on, as many do in their late twenties. I was interested in things that seemed to lie outside the materialistic science that I was teaching, the so-called paranormal phenomena. This is when the synchronicities started happening, as Jayne and I started asking the bigger questions of life. I had read a book called *The Ancient Wisdom: An Outline of Theosophical Teachings* by Annie Besant, which I just happened upon in the town library. It fascinated me that there was this ancient wisdom of a hierarchy of wise beings that were overseeing the evolutionary development of the earth and the human race. Annie Besant was a leading light in the Theosophical Society in the early twentieth century, and the cosmological system described by her made sense to my questing, scientifically trained mind. I started to look into this whole area of Perennial Philosophy, reading books by Helena Blavatsky. Did I believe in God? I think I was pretty much agnostic at this stage, but interested in the idea of a divine presence.

The next synchronicity was when my wife, Jayne, came home one day from her job as a community nurse telling of how the patient she had been treating for a leg ulcer had a daughter who communicated with what she called "Masters". This is a term for those more advanced human beings who had "mastered" their own lower natures and proceeded to guide humanity on its way. The Bible speaks of them in Hebrews 12:1, "We are surrounded by so great a cloud of witnesses". The patient and her daughter had recorded many tapes of the Masters speaking through the daughter. I was very sceptical, but went along to meet them as Jayne was hoping they could help in her healing. Suffice it to say that we were both interested, but also a little apprehensive of what we might be getting into. As a result of this encounter, I started reading the books of Alice A. Bailey, who wrote many volumes in the 1920s to 1940s.

This caused a shift in my understanding. Maybe there were "other beings", other levels of subtle energies not yet discovered by science, other realms of existence. Logically, there was no reason why not. There was a whole raft of human experience, known as extrasensory perception or paranormal psychic phenomena, that was inexplicable by science, including telepathy, precognition, telekinesis, near death experiences, past life recall, remote viewing, and so on. (Remote viewing has actually been used by military intelligence for many years.) It was feasible that one day, science would make the next leap and begin to understand how this realm of human experience worked. (This is the subject of the next book in this series, which looks at how science and spirit are converging in understanding, because that leap is underway.)

The writings of Helena Blavatsky and Alice Bailey presented a whole cosmology of being into which we can fit both science and religion and all metaphysical phenomena in between. It was called the Ageless or Perennial Wisdom (sometimes called Esoteric Philosophy). I was fascinated by it, devoured the books rapidly and started meditating for ten minutes daily using the Great Invocation, a prayer for Light and Love to come down from the Divine realms to fill humanity.

One of the central ideas in Alice Bailey's version of this philosophy is that of Christ-consciousness, an all-pervasive divine energy, which is the highest form of consciousness that we as human beings can attain. We can dip into it during moments of deep contemplative illumination, but rare is the person who can stay there and live everyday life at the same time. It is that of which our soul is made. I began to see that this was the level from which Jesus operated. Now, my image of Jesus at the time had been formed by going to Sunday School until I was nine years old, at which time my father decided to teach me to swim on Sunday mornings. This meant he did not have to go to the dour Presbyterian church we had frequented. My image was of gentle Jesus, meek and mild, someone who loved everybody, except the nasty Pharisees and the evil money changers. It was God in clothes. That was the church image I carried with me into adulthood.

The Jesus I learnt about as an adult was vastly different from my early ideas. As well as reading many Ageless Wisdom texts, I read the Gospels of Mark, Matthew, Luke and John – and learnt about Jesus the Christ. This was a dynamic, enlightened, compassionate, powerful being, capable of healing and giving out deep truths in parable and story form. A true Wisdom teacher. But why was the Christ part of his name only applicable to Jesus in the Bible? Surely Christ-consciousness was for all of us? My wife and I then decided to try out a lively open evangelical church in Leicester, UK. Initially, I was bowled over by the love shown to us. It was not the teaching, the hymns or the words that had an effect, it was the people, their kindness, compassion and genuineness that made a difference. We continued going there, but I was still wondering when the preachers would start telling us about the deeper mysteries, the Christ-consciousness that was available to all.

However, I was soon drawn into the underlying, rigid framework of evangelical Christianity. It does teach transformation through love, but only once you have accepted Jesus as Lord and Saviour and accepted the doctrine of the Church. Everyone else is excluded and, in the starkest teaching, is going to hell or annihilation. I vividly remember, on the encouragement of the church folks, taking all my collection of Ageless Wisdom teaching books and feeding them, one by one, onto the open fire in our house. They were considered the work of the devil in evangelical circles and burnt very well! Strangely, it wasn't until I went off to theological college nine years later to be trained as a Christian priest that I started looking at them again, as several of them were there in the college theological library. A more liberal theology came close to some of their teachings. I eventually wrote a dissertation titled "The New Age Critique of the Church – what can we learn from it?" part of which looked at Christology, Christ Consciousness and the Cosmic Christ. In the subsequent twenty-four years of teaching and preaching as an Anglican vicar in churches large and small, I returned to this theme many times, and in recent years have studied Esoteric Philosophy and the Alice Bailey writings in much more depth. I remain convinced that this gives a much more rounded cosmological picture of who

Jesus the Christ was/is.

The Nicene Jesus

For any traditional Christian, the title of this book is provocative. The Christ and Jesus? Surely Jesus *is* the Christ, there is no difference! Well, my answer would be yes and no. Jesus of Nazareth was a human being. Christ is not a surname and should be expressed as Jesus *the* Christ. The Christ is something much more, much bigger than a flesh-and-blood human. In Christian theological terms the Christ is a third of the Holy Trinity, meaning something of universal, cosmic proportions. How can we reconcile the two? The First Council of Nicaea tackled this in 325 CE and came up with the formula of the Nicene Creed, which was finalised at the First Council of Constantinople in 381 CE. This is the only creed accepted across the board by all major Christian denominations. In it, this is what is said about Jesus Christ:

We believe in one Lord, Jesus Christ,
the only Son of God, eternally begotten of the Father,
God from God, Light from Light, true God from true God,
begotten, not made, of one Being with the Father.
Through him all things were made.
For us and for our salvation he came down from heaven:
by the power of the Holy Spirit he became incarnate from the Virgin
Mary,
and was made man.
For our sake he was crucified under Pontius Pilate;
he suffered death and was buried.
On the third day he rose again in accordance with the Scriptures;
he ascended into heaven and is seated at the right hand of the Father.
He will come again in glory to judge the living and the dead,
and his kingdom will have no end.

Now I'm not going to go into detail about how many of these phrases can be challenged by twenty-first-century understanding, I'm sure you can spot them for yourselves. Huge thick books have been written about what "eternally begotten" means, whether Mary actually was a virgin, what "seated at the right hand of the Father" means and how the second coming can be understood in this day and age. Much of theology stems from literal interpretations rather than understanding these statements in a more metaphorical and mystical light. At the time of these councils, working out an understanding of what it meant for Jesus to be called Son of God was the hot topic of the day for discussion in the streets, much like "Brexit" or the Covid-19 pandemic has been recently. Gregory of Nyssa (335–395 CE) wrote about the theology discussions happening on the streets of Constantinople:

> *Every part of the city is filled with such talk: the alleys, the crossroads, the squares, the avenues. It comes from those who sell clothes, money changers, grocers. If you ask a money changer what the exchange rate is, he will reply with a dissertation on the begotten and the unbegotten. If you enquire about the quality and the price of bread, the baker will reply: "The Father is the greatest and the Son is subject to him". When you ask at the baths if the water is ready, the manager will declare that the Son came forth from nothing. I do not know what name to give to this evil, whether frenzy or madness.*
> (Gregory of Nyssa, "On the Divinity of the Son and the Holy Spirit", in Comby, 1985, p. 94)

Out of that "frenzy or madness" came the Nicene Creed, which has shaped Christianity ever since. Affirmation of the Nicene Creed continues to be the standard by which Church hierarchy judges. If we can affirm the creed, we are okay, if we can't, then we are suspect. Many church-going Christians have told me that they cannot say the creed anymore, or they change parts of it under their breath.

Basically, it was a statement made in the fourth century in order to give a ruling on an issue that was causing contention and unrest then, and it used the mind-set and world-view of the time. We have moved on. It was helpful then, but causes problems for many now. Everything around us has changed. Our understanding of the universe, our insight into human psychology and sociology, our knowledge about health and medicine are all constantly growing and changing. Surely that constant change and development should apply to theology as well as all the other "ologies". A story by Anthony De Mello comes to mind from his book *Song of the Bird*:

When the guru sat down to worship each evening, the ashram cat would get in the way and distract the worshippers. So he ordered that the cat be tied during evening worship. After the guru died, the cat continued to be tied during evening worship. And when the cat expired, another cat was brought to the ashram so that it could be duly tied during evening worship.

Centuries later, learned treatises were written by the guru's scholarly disciples on the liturgical significance of tying up a cat while worship is performed. (De Mello, p. 63)

The Law of Rebirth

So with the idea in mind that there are some "Guru's Cats" lurking in Christian theology, I want to introduce a concept that has been around in spiritual understanding since the beginning, but has been ignored by Christianity. It is the concept of rebirth or reincarnation. In the Wisdom teachings that came via Alice Bailey and others, it is known as the Law of Rebirth. To me, this idea makes much sense and brings a deeper understanding of human life and the cycles of nature. We all know that those natural cycles imply life, death and rebirth. We see it happening every year, as most plants die back during the winter, only to burst forth again in spring. Perennial plants go into a dormant phase, taking stock, rebuilding energies before the next burst of life energy. Annual plants project their seeds to await the next cycle of life as spring comes around again. The nature of this physical universe is such that cycles happen at all levels. Everything is cyclical. Our bodies are ruled by circadian rhythms according to the cycle of the Earth around the Sun. After death, our physical bodies are broken down to their constituent parts by the action of other living beings, to take their part in the next cycle of life. Water, carbon, nitrogen and many other substances all follow biochemical cycles. The positions of the stars in the sky follow cycles. Some of nature's cycles are more like spirals, revisiting but at a higher level as life emerges at ever higher evolutionary forms. If the physical universe happens in cycles at all levels, does that apply to the metaphysical realms as well?

According to Christian theology and the traditions of many other faiths, we have a soul and a spirit as well as a body. A verse often used in funerals is "the dust returns to the ground it came from, and the spirit returns to God who gave it" (Ecclesiastes 12:7). Spirit and Soul are terms used in many different ways, but I think most who believe in an afterlife would say that the part of us that continues on after death is the soul, and the spirit is the divine spark which animates the soul. Traditional Christian theology says that after this one life, there is a divine judgement. But a rebirth scenario would see this as an appraisal and assessment of what has been learnt in one life, in preparation for the next. This places us into a much larger context. The Wisdom tradition says the soul incarnates many, many times on its journey, slowly gaining in understanding of what it means to have life experience in a body, and gradually learning how to use that body for the betterment of humanity. Many people have had the experience of déjà vu, a feeling that we have been somewhere before, or something happens which has been in another time. Dante Gabriel Rosetti captures this sensitively in these lines:

I have been here before,
But where or how I cannot tell;
I know the grass beyond the door
The sweet, keen smell,
The sighing sound; the lights around the shore.
You have been mine before,
How long ago I may not know;
But just when at that swallow's soar
Your neck turned so,
Some veil did fall, I knew it all of yore.

Personality, Soul and Spirit

When I use the term "body", I do not just mean the physical flesh and blood. In the Wisdom teachings, we also have an etheric, energetic body, an emotional body and a mental body, all of which make up the personality: flesh, vitality, feelings and mind. The Wisdom teachings explain that the personality is what we gradually lose after death, but the soul goes on to incarnate again, guided by the spirit. We lose the physical, vital body first, followed gradually by the rest of the personality as it drops away, leaving us as pure soul or consciousness. Each incarnation is a chance to progress the soul journey, and in the next life the soul will be given a personality that is formed in a life situation suitable for its next stage of learning. This is not pointless repetition; the cyclical nature of this is spiral, revisiting the same issues, the same difficulties of being human, but at a higher or finer level. Eventually, the soul will be able to fully infuse the personality, and the person will attain a measure of perfection in physical incarnation. It is a process of progressive development which enables human beings to move forward from totally self-centred survival thinking at a material level to eventual altruistic unconditional love for all beings, and to enter into what Jesus expressed as the kingdom of God, another dimension of being. Human beings in their billions are all at different levels on this journey, and many of those who have gone before us have contributed to the uplifting of humanity from the base expressions of the lower ego-based desire nature to the more enlightened and compassionate members of societies of today.

I know many will question in what way we can say that today's societies are more enlightened than those of the past. But consider these societal behaviours below that used to be acceptable to most of humanity at one stage or other of our evolution. Sadly these activities still do exist – but most of us are at the level of consciousness to recognise them as unacceptable ways of being human.

- Blood sacrifice of children and adults
- Execution by being hung, drawn and quartered or burnt alive
- Genocide
- Torture and execution for the most trivial of offences
- Persecution of minorities, i.e., those not seen as okay
- Slavery
- Patriarchy and domination by men
- Criminalisation of homosexuality
- Child labour
- Capital punishment
- Ecocide

The Law of Cause and Effect

These behaviours are no longer acceptable in many societies, and many societies have moved on from them in the distant past, whilst others are still struggling to rise above them. They were all taken as normal and acceptable behaviour at one time. We are slowly, gradually, one laborious step at a time evolving onto a higher path. The reason for that is that our souls are evolving, and each time we incarnate we learn a little more and work off some more of the past that clings to us. This is the Law of Cause and Effect, known as karma in the East. What goes around comes around. Jesus stated it as "what you sow, so shall you reap". In each incarnation we have to work off some of the harmful effects we have had in previous lives, whilst at the same time trying not to build up more in store for us in the future. There is always an opportunity for change and growth towards more compassion as love draws us on to finer ways of being in each lifetime. It is a vast, complex picture, a huge cosmological puzzle that has many different levels and planes of being. But it does give some meaning to our lives when we wonder, "Why did that happen?" or "What is the point of it all?" We are on a long journey of many lives, the final, ultimate goal of which is to become reunited in conscious awareness in the One Life, the Godhead, the Ground of Being from which we all emerged in spirit. It is important to state that this law, sometimes put as "what goes around comes around" is not a simple "tit-for-tat" response. It is an incredibly complex balancing of forces and influences that comes from way beyond our level of being, far subtler than we could ever understand. It is this which guides our soul in its future incarnations, giving it opportunities to further its evolution in form and progress human consciousness. (More on reincarnation in Chapter Two.)

The Fully Human Jesus

So how does all this metaphysical conjecture speak into the mystery of Jesus and the Christ? Jesus lived in this physical world: he was born of a woman, he grew up with all the hormones and emotions and sexual feelings of puberty and adolescence, he ate, drank, digested and excreted the same as all of us. He must have done as he was fully human. He had a sense of humour and knew grief. He could empathise and love and understand others. I've no doubt he made some mistakes, had a few cross words and other human foibles. This is what it means to be a full human being, with a personality, a soul and a spirit. Some say that the divine spark of the spirit was what he referred to as the Father, as in "the Father and I are one" (John 10.30). The spirit is our channel to the fullness of divinity, the Ground of Being, from which everything emanates, and which holds everything in being. Jesus the man was fully human, and yet as fully divine as a human being could be, meaning that his personality was soul-infused and fully awakened to his divine potential in spirit. He wasn't *more* human than you or me, nor was he a different sort of human. He was a highly evolved human being, and showed us the potential for being human. So what he did is there as a potential for you and me as well, in some future incarnation. The medieval mystic, Meister Eckhart, realised this:

What is the heart of lasting peace in our lives and for the world? Simply this: the realization that what God accomplishes in the only-begotten God does in each one of us as well, so that we might become this beloved one. To what end? So that we might learn to love ourselves, and as we do this, as we learn to love ourselves for who we truly are, we cannot but love everyone else in the same manner. This is the source of wisdom whose end is the peace we were meant to become, which is beyond our understanding but not beyond what we long to know in our experience. (Burrows & Sweeney, p. 63)

Jesus was fulfilling the potential that is there for every one of us, and hence showing us how to love, how to live, how to *be* at the highest level. In living that life, he blazed a path for us all to follow, which is what he called us to do, follow. He never said, "Worship me", but he repeatedly said, "Follow me". In blazing that path, he effected a change in the morphic information field,

17

the collective consciousness of humanity, and cleared the way for all of us to evolve more quickly to higher, finer levels of consciousness. (The theory of morphic fields and information as an underlying pattern will be looked at in detail in the next book in this series, about the science of God.)

So if Jesus was a fully spiritually developed human being in this world, why do we call him the Christ? That will have to wait for Chapter Four. In Chapter Two, I shall explore in more detail the idea of Christian reincarnation or rebirth, and what happened to the idea in the last two thousand years of Christianity.

Questions for Reflection

1. How would you explain why we call him Jesus Christ?
2. What do you feel about reciting the Nicene Creed?
3. In what way do we reap what we sow?

A Practice: The Disidentification Exercise

This is an exercise in disidentifying ourselves from the elements of our personality and beginning to recognise and identify with our higher self or soul. In general, we are so immersed in our feelings and thoughts, or even our physical body, that we miss the nudges of the soul. This exercise will help give balance to your being. (It is a version of a technique developed in Psychosynthesis by Roberto Assagioli.)

Sit in a comfortable position and relax; breathe quietly and slowly for a few breaths, then say:

I have a body, but I am more than my body. I am the one who is aware: the self, the soul. My body may be rested or tired, active or inactive, but I remain the same, the observer at the centre of all my experience. I am aware of my body, but I am more than my body.

Reflect on this for a minute or two and then say:

I have emotions, but I am more than my emotions. My emotions are constantly changing. I recognize that I do not have to change. I have emotions, but I am more than my emotions.

Reflect on this, then say:

I have a mind, but I am more than my mind. My mind thinks constantly in all directions, but I remain the one who is aware, the one who chooses – the one who directs my thinking process. I have a mind, but I am more than that.
(Pause)
I am a centre of pure awareness. I am the one who chooses. I am the self, the soul.

Use this exercise for a few days, and notice any difference it makes in your awareness. Come back to it at regular intervals.

Further Resources
Books

Borg, M. & Wright N.T., 1999. *The Meaning of Jesus: Two Visions*. London: SPCK – two famous theologians with different views present their understanding.

Eastcott, Michal J., 1966. *Jacob's Ladder: An Introductory Approach to the Ageless Wisdom*. Sedlescombe UK: Sundial House Publications

Eastcott, Michal, 1980. *'I' The Story of the Self*. Sedlescombe UK: Sundial House Publications

Websites

"Jesus is not the same as Christ" by Chuck Queen – an article in Baptist News Global, May 7, 2015, https://baptistnews.com/article/jesus-is-not-the-same-as-christ/

Chapter Two

Christian Reincarnation?

I love the word *oxymoron*. It means a figure of speech or phrase in which apparently contradictory terms appear together. Is the idea of Christian Reincarnation an oxymoron? Rebirth or re-embodiment are other terms used. Was reincarnation ever a Christian doctrine? Resurrection is a similar concept of coming back to life after death, but resurrection for us normal mortals is life in another dimension, the spiritual realm termed "heaven" in Christian thought. With the resurrection of Jesus, we find the concept of a dying-and-rising god that is found in several other religions. Reincarnation is a further extension of this, and relies on the understanding that we all have a soul which is on a journey of evolution. After death, the same soul is reborn at some stage and comes back to live in a different body in this physical dimension, in order to progress in its evolutionary journey. I want to emphasise that by reincarnation or rebirth, I mean the soul being placed into another *human* body. The idea that a soul could come back in the form of an animal or other creature is not supported in the Wisdom Teachings.

I don't think the words *Christian* and *Reincarnation* are incompatible. It seems to have been around in the early days of Christianity and some have championed it at various stages in the last two thousand years. Reincarnation is a central tenet of the Indian religions (Hinduism, Buddhism, Jainism and Sikhism) and most varieties of Paganism. In Greek philosophy, we find that Socrates, Plato and Pythagoras also believed in reincarnation. In the Jewish world, reincarnation is an accepted teaching of the Hasidic community and in Kabbalah teachings of Jewish mysticism. The influence of Eastern religions and past life experiences have now placed the issue of reincarnation firmly into the mindset of many free thinkers in the West today. Evidence of child geniuses, the sense of déjà vu, hypnotic regression and past-life recall are all quoted in support. It is increasingly common for people in Western Europe to embrace reincarnation as a way of making sense of life. Surveys reveal about a quarter to a half of those in the "West" believe in reincarnation. As an inter-faith issue, if reincarnation is seen as a totally false understanding of the way things work spiritually, it is very hard for traditional Christian theology to engage positively with many other faiths. Hinduism, Buddhism, Sikhism and Jainism all have reincarnation as a central understanding.

Difficult Questions

Within mainstream Christianity, many find themselves faced with difficult questions about heaven, hell and salvation that could be helped by a belief in reincarnation. The traditional Christian view is that at the end of life we will be judged to be fit to spend eternity in either heaven, heaven preceded by purgatory, or hell. The Reformers excluded purgatory, which makes the division even more stark. Whatever we understand by heaven and hell, this doctrine leaves many questions hanging. How could a merciful God give his people only one opportunity to get to heaven? Is it not inconsistent for an all-loving God to consign living beings to hell after only one chance to redeem themselves? Loving parents will give their wayward offspring as many opportunities as possible to come back to them. Is God's love less than that of a loving parent? Questions like this abound around the doctrines of salvation, judgement, resurrection, purgatory, paradise, Christ's second coming, hell and heaven. Many of them revolve around the understanding of God as an all-powerful ruler, a doctrine many would challenge today. Doctrines arose in the Middle Ages which were based on an understanding of the universe that is very different from that of today. Reincarnation and all it could offer as a way of understanding the spiritual world was discounted, based on some earlier proclamations of the Church, proclamations which were heavily influenced by political manoeuvres to keep the populace in place.

We shall consider briefly:

- The biblical evidence. Is there any justification for reincarnation within the Bible and Christian tradition? (See the appendix to this chapter for more detailed biblical exposition.)
- The early centuries in theological debate and formulation of church doctrine. Has the Judaeo-Christian tradition always rejected reincarnation, or was it just the Church that imposed its decision in the early centuries for political rather than theological reasons?
- More recent considerations. What are the current issues that are making us re-examine this contentious subject?

Biblical Evidence

Commonplace conceptions of heaven would seem to rule out reincarnation – surely heaven is where we go after some form of judgement, and eternal life follows. But the Bible is not clear on what heaven is, other than being with God. We enter "eternal life" as we leave our body and become aware of our eternal nature as soul. The possibility is simply not touched upon that we may first go before God in some way for a "judgement", or, as seems more likely, a life appraisal, before selecting the circumstances for our next incarnation. It is beyond the biblical perspective, which simply looks at the one life that we all live in the body we currently inhabit.

It has to be said that there is not a great amount of biblical evidence for reincarnation, but it does exist in part. It also has to be said there is not much evidence *against* reincarnation in the Bible, which is most peculiar if it was considered a heresy. It was certainly a common belief in the whole of the Middle East at the time. When we put on theological spectacles which say that reincarnation may be a possibility, we begin to see signs of it in many texts. Space in this chapter prevents a detailed exegesis of each biblical passage, weighing up the arguments, but in an **appendix at the end of this chapter**, I present some obvious considerations which seem to be overlooked by most commentators, because reincarnation is currently still considered "taboo" in Church circles. It has to be honestly stated that the evidence is not huge, and the verses can mostly be interpreted in other ways as well. But reincarnation is not the scriptural impossibility we have been led to believe and the Bible does not rule it out.

The difficulty is that the Bible does not say much about what happens after death, and what it does say can be interpreted in many different ways. The words of Jesus, as recorded in the gospels, indicate a concern to encourage people to live in right relationships with God and each other, and to seek the kingdom of God as a hidden treasure, something to be lived out in the here and now, with the promise of eternal or timeless life to come. He was not so concerned about imparting any definitive teaching about the afterlife, about what eternal life was to be, other than being with God. If eternal life is something which is "dipped into" in between incarnations, it is not mentioned in the Bible. We have also to remember that the words of Jesus in the gospels may have been given a gloss, reshaped and added to as time passed. They were written down from forty to seventy years after his death. Who could accurately remember the exact words of someone who died that long ago? Who would not be tempted to embellish their words slightly?

One difficulty is that the Church's understanding of salvation has been so underpinned with the idea of one life, one chance to turn to Christ, that any attempt at inclusion of the idea of reincarnation has knock-on effects for many other of the major doctrines of the Church. It calls for a major overhaul of Christian theology, which has been gradually happening in some academic spheres in the last century and has percolated to the people in the pews in some areas, but has not yet penetrated the Church institutions. It is a paradigm shift, a change in world-view which some have adopted and others are just glimpsing.

Early Church Evidence

Reincarnation has not always been so unacceptable to Church doctrine. In the early Church, as doctrinal matters were being formulated, there was a vigorous debate about the pre-existence of souls and transmigration of souls (reincarnation). Some of the early Church Fathers, such as Clement of Alexandria (150–215 CE), Justin Martyr (100–165 CE), Gregory of Nyssa (330–395 CE), Arnobius (d. circa 330 CE), and Jerome (342–420 CE) considered reincarnationist thinking and did believe in the pre-existence of souls. Reincarnation was a common Greek belief at the time and was discussed as a Christian possibility, especially by those with some knowledge of Greek philosophy, but it was not adopted officially. Even St Augustine of Hippo, in his *Confessions*, entertained the possibility of reincarnation:

> *Did my infancy come after any age of mine which died before? Was it that which I passed in my mother's womb? … And what was even before that, God my delight? Was I anywhere or anybody?* (Blaiklock, 1983, p. 20)

The most outspoken and influential early Christian theologian in this area was Origen (185–254 CE). He was one of the most prolific Church Fathers. St Jerome said of him that he was the greatest teacher of the Church after the apostles, and St Gregory of Nyssa honoured him as "the prince of Christian learning in the third century". Origen certainly believed in the pre-existence of souls and conjectured about reincarnation on numerous occasions. Unfortunately, most of his copious works were destroyed after 553 CE (see below) and we only learn about them from his critics. Jerome, a leading Church Father in the early fifth century, argued that Origen held to reincarnation, or the "transmigration of souls". Although Origen may have believed in reincarnation for some of his lifetime, it seems he may have recanted later, perhaps under some pressure from church authorities. He had his supporters, however, and "Origenism" became hotly debated after his death. It was condemned first at a Council in Alexandria in 400 CE. In 543, Emperor Justinian I condemned Origen as a heretic and ordered all his writings to be burned. Then later, at the Second Council of Constantinople in 553 CE (also known as the Fifth Ecumenical Council), this was said:

> If anyone asserts the fabulous pre-existence of souls and the monstrous restoration which follows from it, let him be anathema.

The "monstrous restoration" was the idea of rebirth of the soul. However, it is thought that there were some political manoeuvrings going on here. This was one of many condemnatory "anathemas" that were largely politically inspired by Emperor Justinian. In order to make "good citizens", it was thought best that the people believe they had only one life, then were destined for either heaven or hell. This would focus them more productively in life and help the empire in its purpose of gaining secular power. Pope Vigilius actually refused to attend on the final day, and seemed, in himself, to be mixed about Origen's views. Some say the anathemas were never officially recognised by the Pope and therefore the Christian Church. Some New Age writers go on to claim that the Church then removed any biblical references to reincarnation, but there seems no definite evidence for this and there are many manuscripts surviving from before 553 CE which indicate otherwise.

Since 553 CE, the rumour of Christian reincarnation has been kept alive by many through the ages as an inner, esoteric core of the Christian mysteries. In the Middle Ages, it was kept alive by the Cathars and the Albigenses, both of whom the Church persecuted for their beliefs. St Anselm was known to be a great admirer of Plato, who taught pre-existence and transmigration of souls, and he is said to have been wrestling with the problem of the origin of souls even on his deathbed. Pre-existence of the soul was taught in post-reformation England by Anglican clergy Henry More, Joseph Glanvill and by William Law in his later years. In the mystical tradition, there are many who would embrace reincarnation, such as Jacob Boehme and Meister Eckhart.

More Recent Considerations

In the twentieth century, Alice Bailey's many works from the 1920s to 1940s have given a whole spiritual hierarchy and cosmology which uses much Christian terminology, as she came from an Anglican background, but has reincarnation as a central belief. Dr Leslie Weatherhead, one-time president of the Methodist Conference, also taught reincarnation. In his book *The Christian Agnostic* he had a whole chapter on Reincarnation and Renewed Chances. Anglican priest, the Revd Dr Martin Israel, author of many books on prayer, mysticism, meditation and healing, sees reincarnation as giving a much better understanding of the problem of suffering in Christian doctrine. In *The Pain That Heals* (p. 168) he wrote:

> *The value of accepting a past history of the soul, one that precedes its present incarnation, is that it puts suffering in a wider perspective of time, and sees life as a series of lessons, or initiations, into greater sanctity.... It comes about that the karmic retribution of the unenlightened unfolds into the karmic opportunity of the fully awakened. The round of rebirth ceases to be simply a way*

of self-improvement ending in a final state of absorption into the Absolute, but becomes instead the vehicle of healing for all the world's suffering, until all creation enters transfigured into the divine presence.

The Rt Rev Hugh Montefiore, ex-Bishop of Birmingham, wrote about his belief and ways in which he believes it adds to Christianity: In an article in *The Christian Parapsychologist* (Vol 15, no.4, pp.121–125), he begins:

The sad fact is that reincarnation has never been taken seriously or properly investigated by Christian theologians... with the result that it has been rejected without proper consideration.

His conclusion is:

It is impossible to prove that reincarnation takes place. It can, however, be demonstrated that reincarnation is not only possible but probable, and that when it is understood in the ways described in this article, far from creating obstacles to Christianity, it can even show benefits that are in keeping with the nature of God as revealed in Christ.

Some of the benefits of reincarnation which he mentions are:

- What happens to young children who die? The injustice of an undeveloped life cut short has led to different ideas, from the state of "limbo" to the idea that they are "de-created". Reincarnation gives a much more positive view of another chance in another life to attain maturity and potential.
- For those who have not had the chance to develop their potential for other reasons and circumstances, rebirth holds hope for a fuller life again, and would reflect God's

goodness to give another chance.

- For those who have greatly advanced spiritually, there is the possibility that they may return to encourage others, to enlighten them and awaken them to the divine by their example of their way of living.

Dr Geddes MacGregor (no known relation to the author) was the Emeritus Distinguished Professor of Philosophy at the University of Southern California, and wrote over twenty books, one of which is *Reincarnation in Christianity*. In this scholarly work he concludes by thinking about the soul in terms of energy, an energy that can be embodied thousands of times, an energy that grows through the abdication of self-centred power and turning in love to God. He sees that a total absence of that energy would lead to hell, a final extinction. But where there is the slightest budding of the love that puts us in communion with God, then he posits that the energy will seek embodiment through which to love God more.

I see no reason why a Christian should not entertain the suggestion that the re-embodiment should occur over and over again, giving the individual opportunity to grow in the love of God. That re-embodiment I would call reincarnation. (MacGregor, G., 1989, p. 171)

Hans Küng, who died in 2021, was a Swiss Catholic priest, theologian, and author. From 1995 he was president of the Foundation for a Global Ethic. He criticised Christian theologians for rarely taking the question of reincarnation seriously, and asserted that it should be seen as a central issue in Christian theology.

This is just scratching the surface of the number of Christian writers, both lay and clergy, who believed in reincarnation through the ages. In her book *Reincarnation: The Phoenix Fire*

Mystery, Sylvia Cranston details many others, not just from Christianity but including Judaism and Islam, who have supported it. She gives a long list of famous writers, politicians, poets and philosophers from the twentieth century who have espoused reincarnation.

We now live in a world very different from that of the early Church, a global culture, one where much more is known about other beliefs, and there are many different experiences to try to understand. The renewed focus on the Perennial Wisdom teachings and studies of mystery religions has brought an awareness of cosmologies that go far beyond the biblical. Alternative and complementary therapies and healing techniques raise questions about subtle energies as yet undiscovered by science, giving auras and energy centres which may be connected with reincarnation and the outworking of the universal law of cause and effect. Quantum physics gives us questions about consciousness and the existence of the soul as an information field at the level of quantum energy, a field which could possibly be held "in the mind of God", and placed in different physical bodies. Channelled communications from those more spiritually advanced who have ascended from the physical body give insight into spiritual hierarchies which are only hinted at in scripture.

All of this goes beyond what is revealed in the Bible and Christian tradition. It does not dismiss Christian theology any more than Einstein's Theory of Relativity and the development of quantum mechanics dismissed Newtonian physics – it just went further and deeper, giving new understandings and revelations into the nature of the universe. There are spiritual understandings that go further and deeper than Christianity, and reincarnation may be part of that understanding. It does not take away from the basis of a God of love to question whether there is something beyond the traditional Christian doctrine of "one life and then heaven or hell". So much of what we now see in terms of spirituality, cosmology, healing techniques, and experiential evidence makes more sense if reincarnation is taken as a part of the framework of belief.

Implications of Reincarnation

What are the implications of a belief in reincarnation for other areas of Christian theology? A belief in reincarnation opens the door to a Christian cosmology that can embrace and give meaning to most other religions and schools of esoteric thought. The ancient mystery religions and initiations can be seen in the light of growing into Christ-consciousness through many different lives. Jesus the man can be seen as an anointed being, initiated into the Christ-energy, receiving the highest level of "Christhood" in human form, the first fruits for all of humanity to follow. He can be seen, in truth, as the son of God, a human living to the fullest of his potential, imbued with the Spirit of God. We all have that divine spark within, "Christ within you, the hope of glory" (Colossians 1:27), which is our destiny through many lives. Jesus showed the way of loving self-sacrifice that we are all to follow. He was the trailblazer, the way-shower, the Light of the world, illuminating the narrow path for us all. That path is trodden not just in one life, but through many, many lives, holding out the possibility of continuing to grow in other embodiments.

It means a radical new theology of the atonement and the sacraments, moving Christianity away from medieval and early Church interpretations of original sin and substitutionary atonement. This is essentially a form of transaction, in which Jesus dies to "pay for" the sins of the world, bringing the forgiveness of a merciful but just authoritarian God. Reincarnation brings a much closer alignment with the original teachings of Jesus as recorded in the gospels, which were about transformation through love and forgiveness, offering more than one life for that to happen. Atonement theology could embrace the concept of karma, if Jesus' death on the cross is understood as overcoming world karma through love, forgiveness and self-sacrifice ("Father, forgive them, for they know not what they do"), hastening a new consciousness in humanity. Through our own lives of self-sacrifice and love we identify ever more closely with the Christ-consciousness within us, until we can be released from repeated earthly incarnations to go on to further realms of "heaven" or higher planes of consciousness in service to the Divine Plan.

Summary

The Bible is not conclusive about many issues, which has led to many heated debates and differences of opinions during its history. It is not conclusive about what heaven and hell are, about the Holy Trinity, about slavery, women priests, homosexuality, divorce and a myriad of other issues. Christian theology has changed, or is changing its ideas about all these. Reincarnation is not condemned within the Bible, although it was a popular belief at the time of the New Testament. It is simply not addressed. The teaching of Jesus is more focussed on establishing the kingdom of God on earth, about how to live our lives here and now, than giving any detailed teaching on the hereafter (or the "herebefore").

Politically, due to the machinations of Emperor Justinian and the 553 CE council, reincarnation may have had a raw deal back in the sixth century CE, which has affected Christian understanding of it since. Yet, through the last two thousand years, there have been those who have argued for it, written books about it, and pleaded for the Church to listen again to the arguments. To believe in reincarnation is not anti-Christian – it can add greatly to Christianity, strengthening it in many ways, but involving some radical reinterpretations as well. Christianity believes in a doctrine that is quite challenging compared to reincarnation. That belief is resurrection of the dead, that our dead bodies will someday be revived and brought back to life. It is affirmed in the last sentence of the Nicene Creed which says "we look for the resurrection of the dead". The Apostle's Creed says, "I believe in... the resurrection of the body." St Paul speaks of this as a spiritual body rather than a physical one, in which case he seems to be talking about the soul, without physicality.

It is sown a physical body, it is raised a spiritual body. If there is a physical body, there is also a spiritual body. (1 Corinthians 15:44)

However, the Gospel of John portrays Jesus as implying the physical bodies will rise again.

The hour is coming when all who are in their graves will hear his voice and will come out − those who have done good, to the resurrection of life, and those who have done evil, to the resurrection of condemnation. (John 5:28–29)

It seems easier to imagine an immaterial soul leaving the physical body and then later electing to embody into a new human life in reincarnation than to imagine that our dead and rotting, decayed flesh and bones would be brought back to full and pulsing life in resurrection, let alone all those bodies that have been cremated and gone up in smoke. My hope is, in the challenging context and global culture of the twenty-first century, that Christianity can be expanded to begin a serious exploration of reincarnation.

Questions for Reflection
1. What are the main objections to reincarnation that come to mind for you?
2. What are the main attractions of reincarnation for you?
3. Which issues from the above two questions do you feel it would be helpful for you to look into?

4. In what ways would Christian reincarnation be a help or hindrance in dialogue with other faiths?

Further Resources
Books

Cranston, Sylvia, 1994. *Reincarnation: The Phoenix Fire Mystery.* Pasadena: The Theosophical University Press

MacGregor, Geddes, 1989. *Reincarnation in Christianity.* Illinois: Quest Books

Hick, John, 1976. *Death and Eternal Life.* London: Collins, Fount.

Martin Israel, 1992. *The Pain that Heals.* London: Arthur James

Weatherhead, Leslie, 1965. *The Christian Agnostic.* London: Hodder & Stoughton

Websites

For many sites, with arguments both for and against, enter Christian Reincarnation into a search engine. Here are some useful sites.

Belief in Reincarnation and Some Unresolved Questions in Catholic Eschatology by Bradley Malkovsky. https://www.mdpi.com/2077-1444/8/9/176/htm.

Reincarnation Evidence of the Afterlife. https://near-death.com/reincarnation – this has a comprehensive view of the arguments for reincarnation.

*Medieval Sourcebook: Fifth Ecumenical Council: Constantinople II, 553_*www.fordham.edu/halsall/basis/const2.html –some fine detail here of the political machinations at this Council which issued the anathemas against Origen.

Appendix to Chapter 2

Reincarnation and the Bible

The Bible is not clear about reincarnation. There are some hints, some intimations, but nothing definitive. Here is a look at the main points in support of rebirth.

1. Elijah and John the Baptist

One of the major scriptural arguments for reincarnation centres around the Elijah and John the Baptist debate. This stems from the book of Malachi in the Hebrew Scriptures, looking ahead to the last days:

> *See, I will send you the prophet Elijah before that great and dreadful day of the LORD comes.* (Malachi 4:5)

These verses were taken by Matthew, Mark and Luke and woven into the story of John the Baptist and who Jesus was said to be. How was the prophet Elijah to be sent? In Luke, the angel Gabriel speaks to John's father:

> *And he will go on before the Lord, in the spirit and power of Elijah.* (Luke 1:17)

"In the spirit and power of Elijah" sounds like a perfectly reasonable description of reincarnation, the same spirit and soul that inhabited the body of Elijah coming into another incarnation in John.

According to Matthew, Jesus spoke clearly to identify John with Elijah:

> *For all the prophets and the law prophesied until John came; And if you are willing to accept it, he is Elijah who is to come. Let anyone*

with ears listen! (Matthew 11:13–15)

"But I tell you that Elijah has already come, and they did not recognize him, but they did to him whatever they pleased. So also the Son of Man is about to suffer at their hands." Then the disciples understood that he was speaking to them about John the Baptist. (Matthew 17:12–13)

Jesus is clearly talking about reincarnation, meaning, "For those who understand about these things, John the Baptist was also an incarnation of the spirit in Elijah." John the Baptist himself did not see it this way, as evidenced by his denial of being Elijah in John 1:21. However, all this shows is that John was unaware himself, as virtually all of us are, of any of his previous incarnations.

This line of thinking can also be seen in Matthew 16, 13–14, 17:9–13, and Luke 9:7–9. Jewish leaders and people of the time were asking the question, "Who are you – are you Elijah come back to us?", which implies a commonplace belief in reincarnation. This is not surprising, as Israel was a cosmopolitan place, a through route by land from Egypt to Babylon, Persia, Greece and Rome, and had been exposed for hundreds of years to various Eastern mystery religions, Hinduism, Buddhism and elements of Jewish mysticism. Reincarnation was not denied and seemed to be assumed, but was just not affirmed clearly in biblical texts.

2. Born Again?
Other words of Jesus in John's gospel can also be seen afresh in the light of reincarnation. In his discourse with Nicodemus (John 3:5–7), what exactly does Jesus mean by being "born again"?

Jesus replied, "Very truly I tell you, no one can see the kingdom of God unless they are born again." "How can someone be born when they are old?" Nicodemus asked. "Surely they cannot enter a second time into their mother's womb to be born!" Jesus answered, "Very truly I tell you, no one can enter the kingdom of God unless they are born of water and the Spirit. Flesh gives birth to flesh, but the Spirit gives birth to spirit. You should not be surprised at my saying, 'You must be born again.'" (John 3:3–7, NIV)

The word translated as "again" from Greek can have several meanings: again, anew, from above, or from the beginning. Traditionally, this is taken to mean a spiritual re-birth – we must be born "again", or "anew", or "from above" to enter the kingdom of God. Is this just a spiritual renewal, or is it another life? Again, there is no definitive answer. But it could be taken that Jesus is saying that this one life is not enough, there is too much for you to become, you must be born anew to continue the journey of your soul in another body.

3. Sin in previous lives?

And as he was passing by, he saw a man blind from birth. And his disciples asked him, "Rabbi, who has sinned, this man or his parents, that he should be born blind?" Jesus answered, "Neither has this man sinned, nor his parents, but the works of God were to be made manifest in him." (John 9:1)

In this passage, given the fact that the man has been blind from birth, we are confronted with a provocative question. When could he have made such transgressions as to make him blind at birth? The obvious answer is in a previous life. The question, as posed by the disciples, presupposes existence in another life before birth, unless there is some way a foetus could be construed to have sinned in the womb, or the doctrine of original sin is pushed to its limits. It will also be noted that

Jesus says nothing to dispel or correct the presupposition. He simply gives another reason, that he was born blind so that he could be healed. This sort of situation would have been an ideal opportunity to correct the reincarnationist thinking of the disciples if Jesus thought it was wrong.

4. Riches of Future Lives?

There is another possible reference to reincarnation in all three Synoptic Gospels: an indirect reference, yet an unmistakable one. Jesus said:

> No one who has left home or brothers or sisters or mother or father or wife or children or land for me and the gospel will fail to receive a hundred times as much in this present age – homes, brothers, sisters, mothers, children and fields ... and in the age to come, eternal life. (Mark 10:29–30)

Taken literally, outside of the doctrine of reincarnation it is difficult to imagine how such a promise could be fulfilled. In one lifetime, one can only have a single set of real parents, and no one seriously proposes that each of the 70 original disciples, who actually did leave their homes and families, ever received as compensation a hundred wives, a hundred fields, and so on. But it could happen via reincarnation. Of course, it also makes sense when seen as a metaphor and taken to refer to entry into the Christian family, with sharing of possessions and a new spiritual family.

5. Escape from Rebirth?

The following passage in the Book of Hebrews, especially the sentence in bold, is a clear statement of the concept of reincarnation. The writer has just gone through a long list of people who have lived by faith, such as Abel, Enoch, Noah, and Abraham.

*All these people were still living by faith when they died. They did not receive the things promised; they only saw them and welcomed them from a distance. And they admitted that they were aliens and strangers on earth. People who say such things show that they are looking for a country of their own. **If they had been thinking of the country they had left, they would have had opportunity to return.** Instead, they were longing for a better country – a heavenly one. Therefore God is not ashamed to be called their God, for he has prepared a city for them.* (Hebrews 11:13–16)

They all admitted they were "aliens and strangers on earth", meaning they no longer belonged there. This seems to imply that those who have their lives fixed on earthly things, the "country they had left", have to return to the earthly existence in another life. But those who are "longing for a heavenly country" are freed from the cycle of rebirth to be in the "holy city" with God. People cease incarnating on earth once they have finally outgrown earthly things.

6. The Mechanics of Reincarnation

There are Bible verses that are highly suggestive of the "mechanics" of reincarnation. Before his arrest, Jesus stated:

All who take the sword will perish by the sword. (Matthew 26:52)

Common sense tells us that not all people who live "by the sword" will die by the sword. This statement can only be true if meant in the context of a future life. If in this life you "live by the sword", you will most certainly die "by the sword", if not in the same life then in a future life. In fact, this concept is the ancient doctrine of "karma" as it is known in the East. We see it expressed in Galatians 6:7 in that we will reap what we sow. This is normally taken to refer to this life only – but makes perfect sense with the law of cause and effect, or karma. This way of thinking is present in a number of other Bible verses, such as Exodus 21:24–25, Matthew 5:25–26, 18: 34–35, Revelation 13:10.

7. An Argument Against Reincarnation?

In the New Testament, one verse in particular is often used to refute reincarnation:

> [M]an is destined to die once, and after that to face judgement....
> (Hebrews 9:27)

This is often assumed, reasonably enough, to declare that each human being lives once as a mortal on earth, dies once, and then faces judgement. Reincarnation assumes that the soul leaves the body at death, faces a form of "judgement" which I prefer to think of as a "life appraisal", and then can enter a new and different body at a later time, to continue its growth in consciousness. The verse implies one body/one death, which does not refute reincarnation at all as it also says one body, one death – and then another body and another death, and so on. But this verse does refute some concepts of bodily resurrection. It was a late development of Jewish thought in the Hebrew Scriptures, which held that after a body dies, the *same physical body* will rise from the grave at a later day to face possible death again and judgement. The resurrection of the body is a gruesome thought and would involve the collection and revivifying of the material particles of the dead body, flesh, bones and blood. This seems totally impossible, given that the elements of the body will have been devoured by fungi and bacteria and recycled into other living creatures. So it is not reincarnation that is refuted, but a bodily resurrection.

8. Other Scriptural Support

There are many other Bible verses that are difficult to make sense of without a belief in reincarnation. Ephesians 1:4 raises the question of pre-existence and predestination:

He chose us in him before the foundation of the world, that we should be holy and blameless in his sight. In love he predestined us to be adopted as his sons through Jesus Christ. (Ephesians 1:4)

How we can be predestined before we exist is difficult to understand, but if we are destined as souls to undergo many different bodily incarnations to prepare us for this one, then it becomes much clearer.

Malachi 1:2–3 and Romans 9:11–13 both state that God loved Jacob, but hated Esau even before they were born. These verses are highly suggestive of pre-existence. In the Wisdom of Solomon, canonically recognised by the Roman Catholic and Orthodox Churches, is the following verse:

I was given a sound body to live in because I was already good. (Wisdom of Solomon 8:19–20)

Surely a person can only be "good" before they are given a body if they were in a previous incarnation.

In the book of Job, we find him making this statement:

Naked I came from my mother's womb, and naked I shall return there. (Job 1:21)

One wonders how that might happen. The only way a person can return to his mother's womb is by rebirth, with a different mother.

These are some of the biblical texts that give some support to the notion of reincarnation. As I have already stated, the Biblical evidence is inconclusive, but suggestive that reincarnation was accepted by many at the time, and not refuted by Jesus. The gospels make it clear that Jesus gave out a more exoteric teaching to the masses, and then an inner or esoteric teaching to the disciples, as much as they could take. And yet, there was more. In John 16:12 he is portrayed as telling his disciples, "I have yet many things to say to you, but you cannot bear them now." Maybe it is time for reincarnation to become exoteric within Christianity.

Note: a very good online article on this topic can be found at https://www.mdpi.com/2077-1444/8/9/176/htm. It is titled "Belief in Reincarnation and Some Unresolved Questions in Catholic Eschatology" by Bradley Malkovsky.

Another good article, based in the Wisdom teachings, is "Reincarnation and Christianity" by Geoffrey Hodson, at www.theosophical.org/files/resources/articles/ReincarnationChristianity.pdf

Chapter Three

Flesh and Blood Jesus

Galilee

I grew up, like most, with the idea that Jesus was from a poor family, eking out a living in a tiny village in the middle of a cultural backwater in the hills of Galilee. How wrong that is! Where was Nazareth? This has a significant bearing on how we think Jesus was brought up and what he might have learnt in his years in the little village of Nazareth. It must have been a small place, as there is no record of it in contemporary lists of towns in the area. This has led some to surmise that it didn't exist at the time, but that seems to me to be ignoring the idea that it was just a little village which later developed into something larger. Its location, however, was only about four miles, an hour's walk, from Sepphoris, Galilee's largest city – a fact which is hardly mentioned in Bible commentaries. Sepphoris had been sacked in 4 BCE after Herod the Great's death, so Herod Antipas, his son who became the new governor of Galilee on behalf of the Romans, set about upgrading and rebuilding it during the time of Jesus' childhood and early adulthood.

Several scholars have suggested that Jesus, while working as a craftsman in Nazareth, may have travelled to Sepphoris to work, presumably with his father and brothers. They were probably stonemasons as well as carpenters, as the Greek word *tekton*, used in the New Testament, was a common term for an artisan or craftsman, not just a carpenter. The term also could mean a mason, builder, teacher, or even engineer, and stone masons were needed in Sepphoris. They may even have been a quite wealthy family of masons and carpenters. The contemporary historian Josephus, called Sepphoris the "Jewel of Galilee," and Herod Antipas selected it as the provincial capital for his government in Galilee. Excavations have revealed a cosmopolitan city of great affluence, with a Roman theatre built into the eastern side of the hill that held over 4,000 people.

Nazareth was also near major international trade routes that connected Africa, Europe and Asia, and during the rebuilding the area would have been a busy hub that employed many people in Jesus' day, sparking an economic boom for the entire Galilee area. Although the population was predominantly Jewish, many people there spoke Greek as it was a Roman province. The whole area from there to Capernaum on the Sea of Galilee, where Jesus moved to later, was certainly not a country backwater, it was more of an international hub, a nexus of trade, and with the traders came new ideas, different beliefs, and exposure to mind-broadening concepts. This was the atmosphere of the area in which Jesus grew up.

Growing up in such a cosmopolitan area, Jesus would have been aware of other traditions of faith outside his own Judaism. He certainly would have been aware of ideas around rebirth, and the appendix to Chapter Two shows how he did not repudiate his disciples when they came up with ideas implying reincarnation. Applying the theory of reincarnation to Jesus of Nazareth, in order to be as spiritually developed as he was, he must have been a human being of many incarnations, an exalted soul, further on the human journey than the rest of us. The human personality into which he was reborn would be of a higher vibrational level, greatly refined and exalted in its physical, emotional and mental make-up. He was a master of love and wisdom. Yet he was a fully human Jesus, not more than human. He was not a different kind of being to the rest of us. What he was in his humanity is possible for us all, at some future stage.

From Bethlehem to Calvary

The Wisdom teachings speak of the journey of the soul through many incarnations. In each incarnation, the soul gradually gains knowledge of what this physical existence is about, of what it means to be conscious in this materiality. The journey is a gradual increase of influence by the soul over the personality, to eventually gain soul-infusion, which means to get to the point where the personality is able to let go of all its desires and wants, and is of such a rarified vibrational level that becomes infused with the love and compassion of soul and becomes a servant in the Divine Plan. This happens through a series of stages or initiations, which we see modelled in the life of Jesus. His life and death can be interpreted as an archetype for all humanity.

There are five great stages modelled for us in the story of Jesus.

1. The Birth at Bethlehem represents the divinity within humanity, the Christ-child born in the human heart, the human realm. It is symbolising divine spirit entering into this material realm. Theologically, the story of the virgin birth, whether you consider it as a literal or mythological story, is one of a special advanced soul coming down from a higher state to inhabit a life on earth. Christianity has chosen to interpret this advanced soul as the only-begotten Son of God, not the reincarnation of the soul of a very advanced human being. Metaphorically, the birth represents the awakening of the awareness of divinity in humanity. It is the divine spark of potential within you and me, of which we are not aware until a moment of awakening. Our true nature is as eternal, divine beings, manifested here and now as a particular flesh-and-blood personality. The virgin birth indicates the divine presence within the heart of humanity. The famous quote from Pierre Teilhard de Chardin is: "We are not human beings having a spiritual experience. We are spiritual beings having a human experience."

2. The Baptism in the river Jordan represents the true awakening to the presence of the soul. In Christian terminology, the dove of the Holy Spirit descended on Jesus as he arose from the waters of baptism, along with the affirmation that this was God's Son. For us all, water represents the purification of the human personality in its three aspects: the physical body, the emotional nature and the mind. At moments of awakening, we become aware that we are not the egoic personality self we thought we were, but that we are one with divine being, a radiance of consciousness coming into form. This is true Self, the Soul. Yet we are not there fully. Following the baptism, Jesus goes into the wilderness and undergoes and resists the temptations. This happens to us all after awakening. Some of us, like the seeds in the parable of the sower, are choked by the thorns on the path of life, or are starved of nourishment in poor soil.

> And he told them many things in parables, saying: "Listen! A sower went out to sow. And as he sowed, some seeds fell on the path, and the birds came and ate them up. Other seeds fell on rocky ground, where they did not have much soil, and they sprang up quickly, since they had no depth of soil. But when the sun rose, they were scorched; and since they had no root, they withered away. Other seeds fell among thorns, and the thorns grew up and choked them. Other seeds fell on good soil and brought forth grain, some a hundredfold, some sixty, some thirty. Let anyone with ears listen!" (Matthew 13:3–9)

Do we have ears to listen? The path of awakening is not easy, and we are given much help and many opportunities to progressively awaken in each life. Realizing who we truly are is one thing, but being able to live it is something else entirely. The trials and tribulations of life are challenging but each is an opportunity for growth, helping us to gradually refine our mental and emotional bodies in particular. The path is long, but it is inevitable. It is brought about by the magnetic attraction of Divine Love, drawing all back to itself.

Your task is not to seek for love, but merely to seek and find all the barriers within yourself that you have built against it. (Rumi)

3. The Transfiguration on Mount Carmel represents the revelation of the true nature of the human being, the radiance that emanates if our perception is opened and our inner eye really sees. We are all divine radiant energy. Science now tells us we are composed of a swirling, vibrational, interconnected nexus of energies, interacting with each other at all sorts of levels. Wisdom teaching tells us that there is a level of reality called the etheric, a level underlying the physical. The human etheric body energises and vitalises the physical body. Many know of it as the system of nadis, chakras and the human aura. The etheric energy system is highly complex, comprised of seven main chakras, but actually thousands of chakras that feed life energy to all of the organs, glands, cells and systems for the physical body. The transfiguration is maybe what we would all look like if our scintillating etheric bodies could be seen. The transfiguration of Jesus was the blazing, radiant aura of his perfected etheric body, revealed to Peter, John and James in a moment of true perception. Peter, James and John are sometimes taken metaphorically to represent the physical body, the emotional body and the mental body, witnessing and awakening to the True Self. In the Bible passage, two other people are there as well, Moses and Elijah, representing two others who reached an exalted stage of godly revelation on mountaintops, Moses on Mt Sinai (Exodus 19:3) and Elijah on Mt Horeb (1 Kings 19:11).

4. The Crucifixion was the culmination of the surrender of Jesus and his non-reactiveness to the desires of his personality nature. He surrendered in humility to the process of soul development, to the persecution of the authorities and to the rejection of the people. He did not object, was silent to the accusations and remained in control of his lower self. His skin was flayed in the lashes. His hands and feet were in agony from the nails. There on the cross, his body cried out for relief. Yet his concern was for those who put him there, that they might be forgiven as they knew not what they had done. Our own path is that we have our own cross to bear, treading our own path to crucify the lower, selfish, desire nature and rise to be centred in a higher nature of love and compassion.

He called the crowd with his disciples, and said to them, "If any want to become my followers, let them deny themselves and take up their cross and follow me." (Mark 8:34)

Jesus' crucifixion gives us a metaphor for our own journey of letting go of the personality and centring ourselves in soul-awareness. The saying "we must die before we die" is the idea that we have to progressively die to our self-centred personalities before the final letting go of the physical plane.

5. The Resurrection and Ascension both showed that Jesus, in his crucifixion and physical death, had risen to such a level of soul-awareness that he could bring himself back to this material world in a body for a purpose, which was to inspire his followers to take his message of love out to the world. In the resurrection stories, he could appear in the middle of locked rooms, show his wounds, appear with different features on the road to Emmaus, eat with his friends, and eventually resolve this post-resurrection body back into the more subtle level it came from at the Ascension. Some of these feats are known of in the East (called "siddhis"), and are demonstrated after years of spiritual discipline and devotion by some. They are potentials within the human form if the consciousness is sufficiently developed and refined. But the teaching is that they are not to be sought after, they will arise when the time is right for each of us as individuals, which for most of us is much further down the line of spiritual development! The resurrection body of Jesus was more than the demonstration of siddhis, it was displaying total mastery of physical form, the ability to manifest at will for the good of humanity.

Awakening

For most of us, we are in the early stages of initiation. The experience of so many people is of an awakening, a moment where the doors of perception open and we realise there is another, higher reality. There can be a brief, tantalising moment of wonder during which light dawns, and we stand on the threshold of a doorway to light and love. It is when our personality gets a glimpse of the soul, our higher being, and realises that there is something more, something inexplicably, immeasurably more, which words cannot explain sufficiently. The doorway has opened to love, the divine energy of the universe. The Gospel of Thomas puts it this way:

> *Jesus said, "Those who seek should not stop seeking until they find. When they find, they will be disturbed. When they are disturbed, they will marvel, and will reign over all."* (Gospel of Thomas, saying 2)

This awakening may have definite stages, but is often a gradual process and can happen through the depths of various experiences we human beings may undergo. Great suffering, death and grief, overwhelming love, awe and wonder, and transcendent visions can all break through the barrier of the pattern of reality that keeps us held down in a state of separation and anxiety. For some, the breakthrough is overwhelming, and they withdraw to the safety of their smaller existence. For others, it is the beginning of their spiritual journey.

My Awakening

For me, a breakthrough and awakening happened through

great suffering, but it wasn't so much my suffering as that of my wife, Jayne. In my teens, I followed a scientific education, with A-levels in Physics, Maths and Further Maths. I then went on to take a science honours degree. As I was about to depart for University, I started dating Jayne and we were married in 1975 after I finished at university. In her childhood, she had developed some problems with compulsive behaviours, such as handwashing and intrusive and troubling thoughts. She also had what she called "black moods" when nothing felt right and everything was perceived negatively. As a result, she had been referred to the child psychiatry service at nine years old, and then again at sixteen years. When we started dating, she was fifteen and I was eighteen. Over the next ten years, she went through cyclic periods of about four years when this mood of depression and intense anxiety would come over her and everything seemed bleak and overwhelming.

During this time she trained as a nurse and I as a science teacher. I thought her troubles could all be sorted with the right attitude and some psychiatric help, but Jayne was on an inexorable downwards slope. Her depression with obsessive-compulsive disorder increased and elements of existential and illusory thoughts started as well. There came a stage where she was working as a community nurse and I was teaching, and she turned up one day in my school. I was called out of the classroom and had to take her home – she was in a crisis of overwhelm and panic, and had come to the school for me to rescue her. This I tried to do over the next weeks, talking and wrestling at a reasoning level with her obsessive thoughts, yet nothing seemed to help. She remained off work for two years as she went into the depths of an existential crisis. She agreed to go into the local psychiatric hospital and remained there for three months. They tried various tests and different regimes of medication, including a course of electro-convulsive therapy, but little changed. At one stage she attempted suicide with an overdose, but eventually they released her gradually, just for weekends at first, into my care. Yet sometimes I had to take her back in during the weekends due to her extreme overwhelm and attempts at self-harm. Over the following two years, she was in and out of hospital many times.

At one point in this nightmare journey, I got down on my knees and cried out from my depths, "If there is a God, help!" I had tried everything I could and had reached the end of my resources and ability to help her. Day after day I was visiting her in hospital and seeing her in total mental anguish with seemingly no hope of an end to it. That was a major step in my awakening, a breakthrough of humility and awareness of my inability to help the person I loved. It was just one of many subsequent moments of increasing awakening to divine presence and love. This is the gradual birth of the Christ-child in the heart, my awakening to Spirit. Jesus talks of this at-one-ment in the Gospel of John.

> I ask not only on behalf of these [disciples], but also on behalf of those who will believe in me through their word, that they may all be one. As you, Father, are in me and I am in you, may they also be in us, so that the world may believe that you have sent me.... I in them and you in me, that they may become completely one. (John 17:20–23)

At this point, I need to say that Jayne gradually became well and able to function in life again, and both of us embarked on a serious spiritual quest, firstly into esoteric wisdom teachings, finally resulting in our "becoming Christians" in 1983. Jayne's healing and integration has continued over the years, although she recognizes that her path in this lifetime is lovingly and wisely to manage this vulnerability. Because of her honesty and openness about her own suffering, it has enabled her to be a source of help and support for many others needing support with their mental health.

It was in 1983 that I had another awakening, this time into Love. There was a moment when I felt the love of God washing over me in waves, bringing tears of joy and relief, as I had been seeking to know and experience God for weeks. The moment was one of surrender, letting go of my own ego, and entering into another level of reality. The next day I woke up and the world was quite literally transformed. I stepped out of the door of the house and was blown away by the verdant, green aliveness all around me, scintillating life bursting from every green leaf and blade of grass. A veil had been lifted and I could see at another level (I think a glimpse of the etheric). Needless to say, the veil often fell down again in future years, but it is getting thinner and gets lifted more often as I progress on the path (and the same is so for Jayne, thankfully!).

Many millions around the world, in all faiths and spiritual traditions, are now awakened and actively seeking to make this world a better place. It is the loving purpose of the One Life we call God, working through humanity. The Wisdom teachings tell us that humanity itself, as a whole entity, is beginning to go through this first initiation process, awakening human consciousness to the touch of the soul and the reality of more subtle realms. Part of this is the upheaval and overturning of ways of being that no longer serve the purpose.

Many ideologies and beliefs have come and gone in the past. They reach a stage in which the thought-forms that contain them are no longer serving the purpose of evolving and progressing the consciousness of the human race, so the energy behind them is gradually withdrawn and the institutions and organizations that are supported by these thought-forms lose their power and strength. We see this happening now in politics, education, religions, and economics. It is a change in world-view, a paradigm shift happening across the globe, in one area after another.

Son of God, Son of Man

But I digress! Why am I not affirming Jesus Christ as the only-begotten Son of God, begotten not made, sitting at the right hand of God? It is not really that I disagree with this, it is that the wording does not mean anything sensible to me anymore. It is mixing up Jesus, with Christ, with the Son of God, and whilst these three terms all overlap, I do not think they are all exactly the same. The term Jesus used to describe himself was *ben-'adam*, the Son of Man, or literally "a son of the human one", which can be translated as the "human being". It has caused theological controversy throughout Christian history, some saying it is another term for Son of God, but in reality, its use in the Hebrew Scriptures was to indicate a human being, particularly in the Book of Ezekiel. Jesus referred to himself over eighty times among the four gospels using the term *ben-'adam*. It was his favoured term of reference for himself, emphasising that he was the same as us, a mortal human being, presenting us with what we could become.

Did Jesus ever call himself the Son of God? No, not directly. Others reportedly called him that, such as Nathaniel (John 1:49) and he did not deny it, but what was meant by it in his day and age? The terms "sons of God" and "son of God" appear frequently in Jewish literature. Leaders of the people, kings and princes were called sons of God. It signified someone with a special relationship with God. At times the whole Jewish nation was referred to as the Son of God (Exodus 4:22). Even angels were sometimes called sons of God (Job 1:6). When his contemporaries called him that, it was before his death on the cross, before the resurrection, before Paul's writings, before any of the gospels were written, and well before the church councils that ruled on what it meant to them later. In his lifetime, it simply meant someone with a special relationship with God, the Messiah, the king or leader who many thought was going to deliver them from Roman rule and establish the nation of Israel once more. The capitalization of the "s" on Son with reference to Jesus is simply a convention of Bible translators. It does not appear in the original Greek or Hebrew, which is all in capitals! The Greek word used could equally be translated as "child".

Nobody ever said to Jesus that he was the *only* son of God. That is the later theological development and assumption by the early church. To say he is the "only-begotten Son of God" is to agree with winners of the controversy that was settled by the Nicene Creed, the first official creed of the early Christian church, which was eventually adopted by, or imposed upon, all branches of the Church. Any other belief was then labelled as heresy. It has become the benchmark of official Christian belief, but many of the terms used in it are so remote from our understanding in the world of today that they are almost meaningless. Each phrase, if looked into, stirs up a hornets' nest of ideas and opinions within Christian theology, but these debates are remote from life today. In addition, the Nicene Creed does nothing to explain what the Christian life should be about, how we are to lead our lives. It is simply a statement of belief, not behavioural intent.

Checking Me Out

At one stage in my vocation as a Christian priest, after publication of my first book, *Blue Sky God: The Evolution of Science and Christianity*, I was called before the Bishop's representative, the Archdeacon, because two other members of the clergy in the diocese had accused me of "apostasy", a serious accusation of abandonment of Christian belief. I was asked if I still believed in the Nicene Creed, as mentioned in Chapter One, to which my reply was, "Yes, providing I can interpret it in my own way." That ticked the box and I continued in ministry.

So here is my own Affirmation of Faith, as stated in 2012 in *Blue Sky God*, following a similar pattern to the Nicene Creed. It expresses my belief in terms I can understand.

My Affirmation of Faith

I believe in the God of Creative purpose, the compassionate consciousness in which we live and move and have our being. Mother and Father of us all, we are held in being by God who dwells in us and all creation, and from whom we emanate and emerge. I believe that Jesus the Christ, a son of God, was a fully human being who reached the depths of God-consciousness to become fully divine, and forged a path for the rest of humanity, through the way of self-emptying and compassion. I believe in the Spirit of God, the divine energy working in the world to bring all things to fullness and restoration. I believe in the sacred nature of the Earth and every human being, and that the spiritual journey is one of becoming transformed by love, letting go of the selfish nature, and entering into the compassionate consciousness that is God.

I would probably rewrite some of that again as my awareness increases. The final stanza in the Nicene Creed is: "We believe in one holy catholic and apostolic Church. We acknowledge one baptism for the forgiveness of sins. We look for the resurrection of the dead, and the life of the world to come". I say nothing about the church in this affirmation of mine. To my mind, the church is not the same as the Church (capital C). The official "Church" encompasses several human institutions as it has splintered over the years, whereas the church is the body of people who follow the morals and values espoused by Jesus the Christ. Some may be members of a Church, some may not. Some may even be of other faiths. If they hold to the teaching to love others, to do to others as they would be done to, then they are recognised as followers of the path Jesus trod: "By this everyone will know that you are my disciples, if you have love for one another" (John 13:35).

Also, can we really "look for the resurrection of the dead"? Is that honestly what we believe? Is that a bodily resurrection with corpses rising from the graves, in tatters of skin and bone? That is altogether unbelievable! Most of the constituent parts of the human have already been devoured by microbes and fungi. If not bodily resurrection, what is it? Is it that our soul, the essence of our being, goes on and survives death of the body in some form of continuity of consciousness? Why call that resurrection? It seems to me to be a misnomer to call it that, stemming from an early belief in the first few centuries after Jesus died. It is more like ascension of consciousness to a higher plane of being, before descending into another incarnation at a later stage, i.e., reincarnation or re-embodiment.

I think the biggest problem that has to be addressed within Christianity is the way in which Jesus the human being has been identified totally with the Universal Cosmic Christ who holds the universe in being. They were conflated into Jesus Christ, Son of God. That is what I would like to tease out a little in the next chapter by delving into the Wisdom teachings rather more.

Questions for Reflection

1. How does it change your image of Jesus knowing that he grew up in a cosmopolitan area, exposed to all sorts of religious ideologies?

2. Have you had a story of awakening? Was there a moment or many moments you can identify? Spend a few minutes in reflection on this.

3. What does it mean to be human? Are there potentials that are undeveloped in most of humanity? Who are the exceptional ones? What makes them exceptional?

Further Resources
Books

Bailey, Alice A., 1937. *From Bethlehem to Calvary*. London: Lucis Press (a deeply esoteric book outlining different initations undertaken by Jesus the Christ)

Borg, Marcus J., Wright N.T., 1999. *The Meaning of Jesus: Two Visions*. London SPCK (especially Part 5 "Was Jesus God?")

Borg, Marcus J., 2011. *Speaking Christian: Recovering the Lost Meaning of Christian Words*. London: SPCK (especially Chapter 22 on "The Creeds and the Trinity")

Nouwen, Henry J., 1990. *The Way of the Heart*. London: Daybreak, Darton Longman and Todd

Vermes, Geza, 2000. *The Changing Faces of Jesus*. New York: Viking Compass, Penguin Putnam Inc.

Websites

Wikipedia has a good article on Son of Man, with many links to other pages.

Chapter Four

The Universal Cosmic Christ

My understanding of who Jesus was and what the Christ is has changed radically over the years. I was what many would call a born-again, bible-believing, crusading Christian at the beginning. I remember having some friends around for a meal and telling them of the benefits of my fundamental beliefs, only to be rebuffed by being called arrogant and deluded! Having previously delved into all the wisdom teachings, I was then told by Christian leaders to reject it all as satanic, and as mentioned before I remember sitting in front of a blazing fire, slowly feeding all my books by Bailey and Blavatsky into it. I was a bit brainwashed by evangelical Christianity for a few years. But the questions kept coming back. Who was Jesus? Was Christ-consciousness something for us all to aim for? How can we understand this Christ? Gradually, over the years, I've pieced it all together in a way that makes sense to me. I hope it does for you too. It is rediscovering the inner mystical tradition within the heart of Christianity that has helped me to join things up, alongside the practice of meditation in the Christian tradition.

Anointed One

Christ (from Greek) and Messiah (from Hebrew) both mean "anointed one", stemming from the idea that the Holy Spirit touched or anointed certain people to serve God. They were anointed with oil to symbolise this spiritual anointing. They were considered "holy", meaning *set aside* to serve God. This was the idea of "Christ" at the time of Jesus. Mark's gospel tells us of Jesus being anointed on his head with expensive oil by a woman in Bethany, which we assume was Mary of Bethany (Mark 14:3), who may have been Mary Magdalene. Jesus was also seen by some as the Christ/Messiah who might save them from the Romans and restore Israel, presumably by some form of revolt and insurrection. His designation as *Son of God* was a direct challenge to the authority of Rome, for whom the emperor was called the Son of God. As a result, he got into trouble with the authorities – and we all know the outcome of that. However, by the time the gospels were written, from forty to seventy years later, the idea of the Christ had taken on much greater proportions, evolving from a person with a special touch of God's Spirit, to the One who sits at God's right hand, to the eternal Logos through whom all was created. A significant elevation indeed!

Holy Oils

I worked for twenty-four years as a full-time Anglican priest, the last thirteen of them in the Church in Wales. In a little-known ceremony outside of clergy circles, the clergy would be summoned by the bishop during Holy Week, usually on Maundy Thursday, to renew their priestly vows. During that service, the anointing oils were blessed. There were three types of oil, one for anointing before baptism, one for use during prayers for the healing of the sick, and one, the oil of Chrism, which is used for various purposes to do with making holy or setting apart for service. It can be used during confirmation services, it is also part of the service of coronation of the British monarch, and it is often used for consecrating buildings, altars and other holy items. It signifies a special presence of the Holy Spirit. The Gelasian Sacramentary, one of the oldest surviving books of church liturgy, contains this prayer for the consecration of the holy oils by a bishop:

Send forth, O Lord, we beseech thee, thy Holy Spirit the Paraclete from heaven into this fatness of oil, which thou hast deigned to bring forth out of the green wood for the refreshing of mind and

body; and through thy holy benediction may it be for all who anoint
with it, taste it, touch it, a safeguard of mind and body, of soul and
spirit, for the expulsion of all pains, of every infirmity, of every
sickness of mind and body. For with the same thou hast anointed
priests, kings, and prophets and martyrs with this thy chrism,
perfected by thee, O Lord, blessed, abiding within our bowels in
the name of our Lord Jesus Christ.

This is the significance of anointing. It is the outward and
physical sign of what is hopefully an inner and spiritual reality.
The anointed one is consecrated for a purpose. Coming back
to the earliest understanding, the Christ, signified in the oils,
is the anointing, the special touch of God, uniting that person
with the Spirit of God – hence Jesus of Nazareth became the
Christ, in a sense. But "Christing" or becoming like Jesus the
Christ is open to all. Jesus himself is recorded as saying, "The
one who believes in me will also do the works that I do and, in
fact, will do greater works than these" (John 14:12). This has
been a puzzle for Christian theology – how can we be greater
than the *only begotten* Son? In this case, it is traditional theology
that is causing the problem. In defining Jesus the Christ, in the
established creedal statements of the Church, as not just as an
exalted Son of God, but also as the *only begotten* Son, it implies
that no one can be quite like him. However, if the anointing,
or "Christing" is seen as an indication of a more evolved
consciousness, connecting with a power of creation, then there
is a loving Christ-principle drawing us towards the fullness of
the consciousness of God. The lovely thing about truly authentic
enlightened beings is that they never exalt themselves. They
share the love and wisdom of the One Reality with all, that is
their very nature.

The Jesus Puzzle

The puzzle of working out who Jesus was began in the New

Testament writings. As the texts emerged over a period of seventy years or so, more layers were gradually added to the bare bones of the story of the life of Jesus and his followers. The disciples were struggling to work out if he was the anointed one come to save them, the son of God who would lead them out of oppression into freedom, or whether he was a more exalted being, a new revelation of God. What we have today in the gospels and letters is theological interpretation of the initial story. Paul's letters were written first, and concentrate much more on his interpretation and understanding of the experience of Jesus the Christ that he had on the Road to Damascus. There is no story of the life of Jesus in his writings. Mark's gospel came next, followed by the Gospels of Matthew and Luke. These two gospels obviously used Mark as a basis, often creatively enlarging on his account, as well as adding new material, particularly the nativity stories.

John is the last gospel to be written and is quite different. It contains the famous prologue, which states that the eternal Word or Logos became flesh in the person of Jesus. John's gospel also contains all the "I am" statements, which are not in the other gospels, despite them being extremely memorable. Each of these indicates that Jesus identified in some way as being one with God, a divine union of humanity and divinity. An official conclusion was not reached until 325 CE when the Council of Nicaea concluded, under some pressure from the Roman emperor, that Jesus was the "only-begotten Son of God, of one being with the Father". But for the contemporaries of Jesus, he was a man, but a man like no other, a man who presented to them who they were and could become. He held up a mirror and showed them the true potential of the human being, the potential for love and compassion, for self-sacrifice and altruism. He gave them the simple core teaching to love one another, and even to love one's enemies. But that notion of Jesus as a forerunner of what the human race could become was eclipsed as the greater vision of Jesus as the Christ and then the only-begotten Son took over.

Cosmic Christ texts

There are several texts in the New Testament that are taken as referring to the Cosmic or Universal Christ, and not to Jesus the human being.

> *In the beginning was the Word, and the Word was with God, and the Word was God. He was in the beginning with God.* ***All things came into being through him, and without him not one thing came into being****. What has come into being in him was life, and the life was the light of all people.* (John 1:1–4)
>
> *He is the image of the invisible God, the firstborn of all creation;* ***for in him all things in heaven and on earth were created****, things visible and invisible, whether thrones or dominions or rulers or powers — all things have been created through him and for him. He himself is before all things, and in him all things hold together.* (Colossians 1:15–17)
>
> *He [God] has made known to us the mystery of his will, according to his good pleasure that he set forth in Christ, as a plan for the fullness of time,* ***to gather up all things in him,*** *things in heaven and things on earth.* (Ephesians 1:9–10)
>
> *The Son is the radiance of God's glory and the exact representation of his being,* ***sustaining all things*** *by his powerful word. After he had provided purification for sins, he sat down at the right hand of the Majesty in heaven.* (Hebrews 1:3, NIV)

The underlined phrases emphasise that this Cosmic Christ is the first cause, the Being through whom everything was made, and that which holds everything in being, God in creation. This Christ is the cause of all Life in the universe. This Christ is the plan, the blueprint for creation. It was a huge expansion of the idea of Christ as the anointed touch of the Spirit on an individual, to the identification of the Christ in cosmic proportions. The Christ was realised as a much larger concept than just a person, a physically limited human being.

Of course, in the first century, the understanding of the universe did not exist as it does for us today. Theirs was a three-tier universe. Heaven was above the earth, behind the stars. Earth was depicted as having a roof, with the stars set in it, and behind the roof was where God lived, heaven. And below the earth was the underworld, Sheol, the place of the dead. Later, this became depicted as hell. As theology developed, theologians pondered on how to fit Jesus with the Christ, as the two seemed intimately connected. In the end, they simply conflated the two and he became Jesus Christ without any full explanation of what that meant. Debates went on for hundreds of years, with many different views being put forward. A limiting factor was that if your view didn't correspond with that of the prevailing bishops, you were deemed a heretic, usually with unpleasant consequences. Many theologians have tried to work it out and struggled to explain it, but is has always eluded a full explanation. Jesus the Christ has been experienced by millions, but was not fully explained by Christian theology. The mystics possibly grasped more of the nature of the divine human than any church doctrine explained. Doctrine can guide our path, but true gnosis, true inner knowing has to be experienced on the inside.

The Cosmic View

As our understanding of the vast size of the universe expanded, so the Christian theology of Christ had to expand. In the last one hundred and fifty years, the Cosmic Christ has become understood as the Divine Presence pervading all of creation since the very beginning. This is the recovery of the teaching of some of the early Christian Fathers of the Church and many of the Christian mystics through the centuries. One of the first in modern times was Pierre Teilhard de Chardin (1881–1955), a palaeontologist and Jesuit priest who started his reflections in his teens from the trenches during the First World War and continued developing his ideas in his numerous writings until his death in 1955. For him, Christ was inclusive of all life, all beings and all elements of the cosmos. Christ was much more than the human Jesus. He saw Christ in all things and all things in Christ, which he called *panChristism*. For Teilhard, the whole of creation was involved in an evolutionary development towards ever greater fullness, which he called *Christogenesis*, and the ultimate destination of this was the *Christ-Omega* point, the climax of creation, a point of total synthesis. From 1920 onwards he referred to the Universal Christ as the "organic centre of the entire universe". He understood the words in the Gospel of John, "And the Word became flesh" (John 1:14), to refer to the whole universe, the enfleshment of Christ in all creation. So for Teilhard de Chardin, the Universal Comic Christ was seen in three interconnected ways, as the centre of the universe, the centre of humanity, and the centre of each person. (I'm indebted to Prof Ursula King and her book *Christ in All Things* for these insights from Teilhard de Chardin.)

Matthew Fox provides a similar view in his book *The Coming of the Cosmic Christ*, published in 1988. He bewails the loss of Cosmic Christ theology that was present in the writings of the early church fathers, blaming the church's obsession with Augustinian ideas and the Enlightenment quest for the historical Jesus.

The Enlightenment's quest for the historical Jesus to today's quest for the Cosmic Christ names the paradigm shift that religion and theology need to presently undergo.... The old wineskins of an anthropocentric, rationalistic, antimystical, antimaternal world view cannot contain the new wine of creativity that is exploding wherever minds, hearts, and bodies are being baptised into a living cosmology, into the living Cosmic Christ. (Fox, 1988, p.78–9)

Fox talks of the Cosmic Christ as the "divine *I am* in every creature" and as the "pattern that connects", a pattern permeating all creation. This overlaps with the particle/wave nature of quantum physics. At sub-atomic levels, the matter of which we are made has two states of existence, as both particles and waves. Waves of potential are "smeared out" over space until they are "observed" in materiality. (Much more information on this is given in my previous book, *Blue Sky God*.) Using this as an analogy, the historic Jesus can be seen as the "particle" Christ, an individual materialised in space and time. The Cosmic Christ is the "wave-form", a pattern without boundaries, permeating all creation, an eternal presence drawing everything into an emergent, evolutionary future, the Omega point in Teilhard's thinking. This wave-form of cosmic consciousness or energy pervades everything, and can be sensed in times of deep mystical experience. Leading edge scientists are currently proposing theories of universal consciousness which tie in with spiritual viewpoints and show an emerging convergence between science and spirit.

Universal Christ

More recently, the Franciscan priest, Fr Richard Rohr, in his book *The Universal Christ* (2019), makes what I think is one of the clearest distinctions in his phrase:

Jesus is the union of human and divine in space and time, and the Christ is the eternal union of matter and Spirit from the beginning of time.

In his understanding, the Universal Christ is the eternal divine principle or blueprint through which the reality of God has become manifest in the world. The Christ was the first Plan, and is the eternal union of matter and spirit as one. As such, the whole of creation is the Christ clothed in matter, enfleshed in form. Eventually, through the process of evolution, animal life has reached the stage in humanity where the Christ could be recognised and Jesus became the archetype for us all, the union of human and divine in space and time.

In Rohr's view, wherever the human and the divine coexist, we have the Christ, the anointing with Spirit. Wherever the material and the spiritual coincide, we have the Christ. The Christ is the Divine principle behind all things, that which holds it all in existence. That includes the mineral world, the plant world, and the animal world, including humans. In his own words, he says the Christ "is another name for everything". This blueprint became personified and visible in a human being, Jesus, such that we could see the potential of humanity.

In this understanding, the human Jesus was not born as the Christ, he did not open to the reality of his "Christness" until just before he emerged on the scene as a thirty-year-old male in Galilee. The human Jesus had to undergo a significant transformation, a transmutation, before becoming the anointed one, which is shown biblically as the Holy Spirit descending upon him as a dove at his baptism. This was his initiation into a higher consciousness.

The Wisdom teachings see this from the vantage point of the ages. His soul had been honed through many reincarnations, and was of such purity and fine vibrational quality, that his consciousness opened into the realisation of Oneness with Divinity. The veils of reality fell away, and he could see "all the way up and all the way down". From that moment, his years of ministry started, his wisdom teaching emerged, and his healing powers became evident. Jesus the man became "overlighted" by the Christ-energies. The human and the divine co-existed and he was the Christ in human form, or as much as can be contained within a human form. Yet this Christ, this divine blueprint for all time sustains the whole universe – not just Jesus the human being. As Richard Rohr points out.

> *In the early Christian era, only some Eastern Fathers (such as Origen of Alexandria, Irenaeus, and Maximus the Confessor) noticed that the Christ was clearly something older, larger, and different than Jesus himself. They mystically saw that Jesus is the union of human and divine in space and time; whereas the Christ is the eternal union of matter and Spirit from the beginning of time. In later centuries, the church lost this mystical understanding in favor of fast-food, dualistic Christianity that was easier for the average parish believer to comprehend. We pushed Jesus, and we lost Christ.* (Richard Rohr, Daily Meditations, "The Union of Human and Divine", 6 April 2017)

Rohr has a conversational podcast series called *Another Name for Every Thing with Richard Rohr* which dives deep into his book. Full details are in the Further Resources at the end of this chapter.

Perennial Wisdom Viewpoint

This view of the Universal Christ is very similar to that of the Perennial Wisdom teachings, particularly in the writings of Alice Bailey. The Cosmic Universal Christ or Christ Principle permeates the whole of the cosmos and can be considered as a living unitive field underlying all things. It can be experienced as a dimension that runs through the whole universe and the space-time dimension, right back to the Source, the Godhead, the One Life. It is a dimension as real as space and time, but moving along it allows us to transcend space and time as we know them. It represents the principle of loving unity and wisdom expressed by the One Life (God, the Absolute) through all of Creation. It is the greater Life imbuing all life, binding everything together. It is the magnetic force attracting humanity back to Oneness. It is the Law of Attraction drawing everything into more complex relationships, the magnetic love-force behind evolution. In the human domain, the soul of humanity is the expression of the Christ Principle. In the individual human being, it manifests as selfless love and wisdom, the Christ-consciousness of the soul. When we manifest this Christ-consciousness, we generate qualities of collaboration, cooperation, participation, co-creativity, compassion, and love. The sense of a separate, isolated self evaporates, and we become aware of the oneness of Being. It is, as Jesus described, the kingdom of God made manifest.

The Wisdom teachings say that from primal Divine Nature (the Godhead in Christianity), the Christ emerges by the interaction between the different aspects of the Divine Source, which is beyond all comprehension. This creative Source expresses in three ways as

a) the Cosmic Will or Father aspect, the force of purpose and will, and

b) the Cosmic Intelligence or Mother aspect, the creative intelligence of the Source, the principle of gestation and manifestation of physical substance. (This aspect of the Divine Source emerged in Christian theology as the Holy Spirit, unfortunately male! The female Sophia or Wisdom would have been a better choice. See Proverbs 8 and Chapter Six.)

c) From the Cosmic Will and the Cosmic Intelligence, a third essence is generated, the principle of relationship or Universal compassionate consciousness, the Cosmic Son or Love-Wisdom aspect.

So from within this Trinitarian Source, the principle of relationship is the Universal Christ, which is consciousness itself expressed in beauty, intelligent love, harmony, wisdom, and compassion. This omnipresent consciousness is manifest in patterns of existence at all levels and is seen to be individuated in human beings. In ancient times, this was recognised by anointing with oil, which meant this person is seen to have reached a level of wisdom surpassing that of most people. In Jesus, the love, wisdom, compassion and understanding that flowed from him was recognised as the highest Christ-consciousness that could be attained by another human being, and hence he was seen as divine.

Multilevel Christ

So we begin to see the Christ as a multilevel term. The Universal Christ energy is present throughout the universe, sustaining and developing, holding everything in relational being, even down to the fundamental forces of physics – the gravitational force, the electromagnetic force, the weak nuclear force, and the strong nuclear force. These can all be considered at a deeper level as expressions of the Christ energy. At an ecological Earth level, the Christ is the shining, mystical presence behind nature, holding the life pattern of it all. Why does the acorn develop into the majestic oak tree? Why do the sperm and egg become one cell which replicates to emerge as an incredibly complex mammalian being? Because there is an underlying pattern, an informational blueprint which subtly draws the life into full form. It is the soul, imbued with the Christ energy, the Principle holding all creation. At a human level, the Christ energy is manifest in our depths, and we awaken to it when we open our hearts and minds to universal love.

In the New Testament letters attributed to Paul, he worked hard to explain the Christ presence in humanity in terms of formation and fullness:

My dear children, for whom I am again in the pains of childbirth **until Christ is formed in you**. (Galatians 4:19)

I pray that out of his glorious riches he may strengthen you with power through his Spirit in your inner being, so that Christ may dwell in your hearts through faith. (Ephesians 3:16–17)

God has chosen to make known among the Gentiles the glorious riches of this mystery, which is Christ in you, the hope of glory. (Colossians 1:27)

For in Christ all the fullness of the Deity lives in bodily form, and in Christ you have been brought to fullness. (Colossians 2:9–10)

In this view, Jesus the Christ is the human manifestation of the divine Christ Principle, that divine energy which equipped and enabled him for his years of ministry, teaching and healing. He was the Christ incarnate, the union of human and divine in space and time. But, as previously mentioned, he is quoted as saying in the Gospel of John:

Very truly, I tell you, the one who believes in me will also do the works that I do and, in fact, will do greater works than these, because I am going to the Father. (John 14:12)

This means that the door is open for us all to progress, through many incarnations, to the fullness of Christ, to the exalted level of embodying fully the Christ energy. Jesus was the one who showed us the way, the full human incarnation of Divine Love-Wisdom. In showing the way, he modelled and established the path of transformative love which we can all learn to follow, at our own level.

To clarify, within the Perennial Wisdom teachings we find that there are three aspects to expressing the Christ working in all creation.

1. The Universal Christ/Christ Principle: the third aspect of the Divine which permeates the whole of the cosmos. It is likened to a living unitive field underlying all things. It represents the principle of loving unity and wisdom expressed by the One Life (God, the Absolute) through all of Creation. It is the greater Life imbuing all life, binding everything together. It is the force attracting humanity back to oneness. In the human domain, the soul of humanity is the expression of the Christ Principle. In the individual, it manifests as selfless love and wisdom, as we see in Jesus.

2. The Christ in you is the consciousness of the soul as it progresses through many incarnations. In this regard, we are all Christs in the making. The soul is an expression of the Christ spirit, it is the centre of our spiritual make-up, founded on the principle of selfless love. The soul learns through each incarnation. Each of us is evolving towards a kind of personalised Christhood that embodies the Christ Principle, the Christ consciousness within. Jesus was fully developed in his Christ-consciousness and so Jesus was the Christ in human form. But we are all proto-Christs in the making.

3. The Christ is also an exalted position known as the World Teacher, held by a very advanced being as head of what is termed the Hierarchy. I don't particularly like the term Hierarchy, but it is the term used in the Theosophical branch of the Wisdom teachings. It could possibly be replaced with another term in future. It is said the Hierarchy is a community of advanced, enlightened souls who bear responsibility for the outworking of the Divine energies that manifest in the created universe. They are sometimes called Ascended Masters in the literature, in that they have mastered their lower selves and passed through many initiations to reach an enlightened state. To comply with current gender sensibilities, they are sometimes called the Great Ones. They have the responsibility for guiding humanity through its evolution.

In Christian terminology, the Hierarchy overlaps with terms such as the cloud of witnesses, the communion of saints and the host of heaven. It is those exalted souls plus the angelic beings who all oversee the manifestation of divine energies. These energies enter the consciousness of humanity, and thence into material reality in social structures at all levels. The Hierarchy works for the evolution of humanity through human intuition, sending spiritual energies that we develop into our own thought forms, at our own level of development. It is difficult to represent these ideas without lapsing into thinking in physical terms of human hierarchies and structures. My understanding is that it is all much more ethereal and flowing on the spiritual planes of being.

The holder of the position of Christ or World Teacher oversees the Hierarchy's work and changes with the cycles of time. The current holder is said to be a highly exalted being called Maitreya, responsible for the blending of East and West together. This is the one who is said to have "overlighted" or "overshadowed" the consciousness of Jesus during his ministry years. In doing so, the consciousnesses or souls of both Maitreya and Jesus merged and each made significant advancements in stages of initiation in their own spiritual evolution.

This is a perplexing area for those who have been brought up with the traditional Christian teaching that Jesus is the Christ, and at the beginning of the book I posed the question: "Are the Christ and Jesus the same or different?" My answer was both yes and no. The Christ is a much bigger concept than the human Jesus, yet he was the Christ in human form. But when we consider the multilevel Christ, it raises the next question: "Where is Jesus now if he is not the holder of the Christ position as World Teacher and head of the Hierarchy?" As previously mentioned, according to the various Wisdom Teachings, our souls all progress through a series of initiations in our journey through numerous lives. Most of us are at the first or second initiation stages. During the crucifixion, the more advanced soul of Jesus is said to have undertaken the fourth initiation, and since then has undertaken the fifth and sixth. He is one of the Great Ones, the Ascended Masters, and currently said to have oversight of the whole range of devotional spirituality and religion, not just Christianity but all forms of devotional energies in religion and spirituality.

Making Sense for Today

All this talk of Masters and initiations is a difficult concept if we think of it at the physical, material level of structures in our own societies. Unfortunately, that is the human language we have developed, and words are not adequate for this more subtle level of understanding. We grasp for words to explain, and our default position is always to think of these concepts of exalted beings in terms of our own physical human shape – we anthropomorphize it all. However, my belief is that we need to think far more in terms of the *energy of being* when we think of soul. The energy of being that was at one time called Jesus has incarnated in many other human bodies since and has progressed and developed to take responsibility and oversight of a whole raft of human affairs to do with the energy of devotion within humanity, an energy know as the sixth ray of devotion. Of this ray, William Meader, a contemporary teacher of esoteric philosophy, says,

> *As a major shaping force in human consciousness, devotion to all that is sacred is the essential effect of this Ray. With an accompanying sense of sacrifice and submission, the sixth ray inclines the human heart to demonstrate reverence to that which is deemed good, true and beautiful.*

This is the area of service that the energy of being that was in Jesus of Nazareth is now overseeing for the benefit of humanity.

Summary

Jesus of Nazareth was a human being, but one who had

progressed to a perfected state, fully attaining Christ-consciousness. Anointing with oil was the recognition of a special touch of the Spirit on someone, and anointing is what Christ or Messiah meant in the Hebrew Scriptures. The New Testament contains many passages indicating the Christ is a universal principle of creative loving consciousness, the eternal plan or pattern of existence. This presence was somehow recognized in the human Jesus. In the early Church, theologians worked it all out to their satisfaction in the Nicene Creed, conflating Jesus and the Christ. More recent work has developed the idea of the Cosmic or Universal Christ Principle pervading the whole cosmos, sustaining and undergirding all manifest existence. This manifesting divine energy is suffused within all material reality, evolving it into further becoming. With regard to understanding the subtle difference between Jesus and the Christ, I repeat Richard Rohr's phrase:

Jesus is the union of human and divine in space and time, and the Christ is the eternal union of matter and Spirit from the beginning of time.

Developing in parallel to the Christian notion of Jesus the Christ, the Ageless Wisdom teachings see that energy of being of Jesus of Nazareth merged with that of the Maitreya Christ, such that he became Jesus the Christ during his years of ministry and both beings undertook significant stages of spiritual initiation during the crucifixion and resurrection of Jesus the Christ.

Questions for Reflection

1. How far and in what way do the ideas expressed in the book so far differ from your own thinking about Jesus the Christ? Do you find that disturbing? If so, what aspect is disturbing to you?
2. Should these ideas be introduced to Church teaching?

How could that happen?

3. What would you like to see emerging as a new form of Christianity?

Further Study Resources
Books

Delia, Ilio, 2011. *Emergent Christ: Exploring the Meaning of Catholic in an Evolutionary Universe.* New York: Orbis Books

Fox, Matthew, 1988. *The Coming of the Cosmic Christ.* New York: HarperOne

King, Ursula, 2016. *Christ in All Things.* New York: Orbis Books

MacGregor, Don, 2012. *Blue Sky God: The Evolution of Science and Christianity.* Alresford UK: Circle Books, John Hunt Publishing (particularly Chapter Five, "Rethinking Jesus")

Rohr, Richard, 2019. *The Universal Christ.* London: SPCK

Websites

Richard Rohr's podcast series on the Universal Christ can be accessed via any podcast platform. See cac.org/podcast/another-name-for-every-thing/

Also there is an hour-long talk on his writing of the book on YouTube: https://youtu.be/RY8-l_GQ_IY

Wikipedia has a helpful page on the Cosmic Christ

The Centre for Christogenesis at christogenesis.org promotes Ilia Delio's work and has an interesting article "Reply to Richard Rohr on the Cosmic Christ"

CANA, Christians Awakening to New Awareness, have a good downloadable Study Booklet called *The Christ* by Adrian B. Smith. Find it under the Resources section of www.cana.org.uk

The Integral Christian Network has some good articles about the developments in Christian practice and theology at www.integralchristiannetwork.org/writings

Chapter Five

The Mystical Christ and Oneness

There have always been different versions of Christianity, because we are all different human beings with a variety of perceptions. Many of those different versions have split off from the Roman church over one disputed theological point or another. My roots are in the Anglican tradition, which has been known as a "broad church", holding within it a wide range of theological opinion and belief. Some people take their faith very literally, accepting the Bible as the infallible word of God, not questioning it deeply, happy to have a simple faith. Some want to dig deeper into the meaning and interpretations of the texts to tease out theological nuances. And some have a mystical experience of God or the Universal Christ, of Oneness, of Divine Cosmic Consciousness, which they spend much of the rest of their life trying to work out. Those who see it all from this more mystical perspective have written through the ages in an attempt to express themselves coherently. Much of that writing is about a relationship with the Divine, or the Absolute, about being held in love, and seeing the world differently as a result.

William James in his classic book *The Varieties of Religious Experience* wrote:

In mystic states we both become one with the Absolute and we become aware of our oneness. This is the everlasting and triumphant mystical tradition, hardly altered by differences of clime or creed. In Hinduism, in Neoplatonism, in Sufism, in Christian mysticism, in Whitmanism, we find the same recurring note, so that there is about mystical utterances an eternal unanimity. (James, 1902, p.419)

James considered these personal experiences to be more fundamental than any church teaching or theology, and he saw them as having four definable qualities:

1. Ineffability, in that it is very difficult to put these mystical experiences into words.
2. A noetic quality, in which intuitional insights are gained that go beyond the intellectual or emotional.
3. Transiency, as most of these experiences are short-lived, yet have long-lasting effects.
4. Passivity, as most of these experiences just happen to people, they are not sought out (except for those who take entheogenic substances).

The Mystical Experience

The way I see it is that these mystical experience of oneness are a human experience, something possible for all humanity, given the right conducive circumstances. Not everyone has had that human experience, but for those who have, it is life changing. What is it? It's when we are taken up in a feeling and knowing of such awe and wonder that we know we are one with everything, and are held in love. It is a normal human experience, a unitive, non-dual experience of reality beyond the physical. But that experience is then interpreted in the understanding of the time, culture and context of that person. So the articulation of these experiences tends to take on the clothing of the religious and societal system of the time. The problem is that we often mistake the outer clothing for the inner human experience, which leads us to imagine that there are differences, where actually none exist. It is largely a problem of language and the inadequacy of words to describe mystical experiences. As William James said, mystics have described the same type of experience in the terms of Hinduism, Buddhism, Sufism, Christianity and many other faiths, plus those without any religious affiliation.

I vividly recall a friend who, in a tragic accident, reversed in a tractor over his disabled toddler son and the son died. My friend had no religious faith, but months later described to me how, a few days after his son died, he sat down in complete despair, wondering how he could go on. Then, without any effort on his part, he felt himself being caught up in the most wonderful music and coloured light patterns. Before he knew it a couple of hours had gone by and, when he came back to himself, he had this feeling of conviction that he could carry on in life and was somehow being held through his grief and loss. He could not describe in any detail what had happened to him – he just *knew* it. We cannot imagine the depths of despair he must have felt, and yet he was given the grace to forgive himself and carry on. Suffering can strip us bare, peeling away all our defences, exposing the basis of who we are as a spiritual being having a human experience. Moments of both deep suffering and deep joy have the ability to strip our normal defences back so that the numinous, ineffable compassionate Christ-consciousness can reach our awareness.

My own experiences take me back to 1983 to a moment of transcendence that I mentioned in Chapter Three, when I experienced waves of love crashing over me like a waterfall, and joy was released in my life. It happened quite unexpectedly one evening as I was talking to my wife in bed, but I know it was something to do with me letting go of my controlling self and opening to what may be. After eventual sleep that night, I woke the next morning and stepped out of the door to what I perceived as a new reality. Everything sparkled with life. I had never before seen such vibrant greenness in the plants and trees. Everything was alive and suffused with love and light. A door had opened to my soul and spirit. This sense of elation and joy and new perception lasted for several days, but the lasting effect has been for the rest of my life. At that moment, I awakened into a greater reality.

Clothing the Experience

The clothing that I put onto this mystical experience at the time was that of evangelical Christianity, so I interpreted it as being "born again" in the Holy Spirit. And yet I had already read much of the deeper Wisdom teachings and could also see it being an experience of touching into Christ-consciousness, the Universal Christ. The Gospel of John and the letters of Paul put this into a Christian perspective. In John chapter 14, Jesus talks of going away, but leaving the Spirit, the one who comes alongside, the helper. He gives the assurance that we are all One in Spirit.

> *And I will ask the Father, and he will give you another Advocate, to be with you forever. This is the Spirit of truth, whom the world cannot receive, because it neither sees him nor knows him. You know him, because he abides with you, and he will be in you.... On that day you will know that I am in my Father, and you in me, and I in you.* (John 14:16,17,20)

So the coming of the Holy Spirit was to be the day that they would realise that the Christ, the I AM, was within them. This is really about awakening to the Christ energy-presence all around and within us. It was not fully worked out theology, and in many ways the Holy Spirit is presented as the same as the Spirit of Christ. Paul certainly seems to equate the two:

> *But you are not in the flesh; you are in the Spirit, since the Spirit of God dwells in you. Anyone who does not have the Spirit of Christ does not belong to him.* (Romans 8:9)

If we are aware of Christ-consciousness within us, we are in unity with the Divine, one with God in some deep mystical way. This is recognition of unity with diversity. We are one, yet we are individuals.

*The glory that you have given me I have given them, so that they may be one, as we are one, **I in them and you in me**, that they may **become completely one**.* (John 17:22–23)

St Paul and Mystical Experience

In Galatians 2:20 Paul went even further than saying that Christ was in him, as he maintained that he himself had died.

I have been crucified with Christ and it is no longer I who live, but Christ lives in me. (Galatians 2:20)

He was in effect saying that the self-centred, egotistical, desire nature of his personality was now dead because Christ was in him. He was centred in a different place, a different source of power, coming from a place of compassion and love. From that place, his fervent prayer and wish was that we may all join him in his awakened state.

*I pray that, according to the riches of his glory, he may grant that you may be strengthened in your inner being with power through his Spirit, and that **Christ may dwell in your hearts** through faith, as you are being rooted and grounded in love. I pray that you may have the power to comprehend, with all the saints, what is the breadth and length and height and depth, and to know the love of Christ that surpasses knowledge, so that you may be **filled with all the fullness of God**.* (Ephesians 3:16–19)

The heart in biblical times was understood more as the centre of being, including the mind and emotions and personality. The author (probably not Paul) writes as if Christ is a principle of love rather than a person. We need strengthening so that this way of being, this Christ-consciousness, can be birthed in our hearts. Paul expresses it in his letter to the Colossians:

I became its [the early Church's] servant according to God's commission that was given to me for you, to make the word [Logos] of God fully known, the mystery that has been hidden throughout the ages and generations but has now been revealed to his saints. To them God chose to make known how great among the Gentiles are the riches of the glory of this mystery, which is **Christ in you**, *the hope of glory.* (Colossians 1:25–27)

My goal is that they may be encouraged in heart and united in love, so that they may have the **full riches of complete understanding**, *in order that they may know the mystery of God, namely, Christ, in whom are hidden all the treasures of wisdom and knowledge.* (Colossians 2:2–3, NIV)

This tells us that the Christ the Logos, the Word of God in John's gospel, is identified by Paul as the mystery of God, and is *in you*. This Universal Christ contains the *full understanding* or pattern of everything. It seems to me to imply that the Christ is there in every person, a divine underlying spark in all, because we are sustained in being by this Christ principle. The Bible tells us that all things were created through him and are held in being by him. Traditionally, the new Christian is asked to invite the Christ in, and I think that represents the awakening or opening to the spiritual, when we become spiritually aware. Remember, Paul tells us that:

He is the image of the invisible God, the firstborn of all creation; for in him all things in heaven and on earth were created,... all things have been created through him and for him. He himself is before all things, and in him all things hold together. (Colossians 1:15–17)

Panentheism

So everything is in Christ and Christ is in all, sustaining all.

This is the holographic pattern of all reality, theologically called *panentheism* – God is within all, holding all things in being, and yet is still transcendent, meaning "other" and not meaning "up above". Science speaks of informational patterns to which material reality conforms at every level, the pattern of all existence, and we can see a link there with the idea of the Universal Christ, in which all exists. This is a much bigger concept than Jesus ascending to his Father in heaven. This means that the vastness of the Cosmic Christ was in Jesus, and Jesus awoke to that in the *fullest way possible* for a human being – he became the divine human, the human being who became one with the Christ presence within all. At the depths of our being, we all have a mystical relationship with the One who holds the universe in being – but not all are awakened to that presence and for many it remains hidden and unconscious.

St John of the Cross (1542–1591) made an important distinction between the fundamental union with God which sustains our being, and the union of the soul, through love. In mystical theology, union of the soul with God is the fruit of a journey into love.

> To understand the nature of this union, one should know that God sustains every soul and dwells in it substantially, even though it be the greatest sinner in the world. This union between God and creatures always exists. By it, he conserves their being so that if the union should end, the world would immediately be annihilated and cease to exist....
>
> Consequently, in discussing union with God we are not discussing the substantial union which always exists, but the soul's union and transformation in God that does not always exist, except when there is likeness of love. (St John of the Cross, *The Ascent of Mount Carmel*, 2.5.3)

This distinction is important as it says we all are sustained in being by a fundamental presence of God, but we are not all awakened to the union by love. The Universal Christ is that by which, in which and through which all is created, but it takes a journey into loving Christ-consciousness to awaken to that presence of Oneness. That's the purpose of the spiritual journey of transformation into love; to become aware of the divine presence within.

Oneness through the Ages

Some quotes from sacred and inspired writings will show how this Universal Christ Oneness has been expressed for thousands of years. It has been said by the few, but not heard by most, or, if heard, not really believed. In different faiths, using different terminology, the same One presence is described. And now, science is beginning to say the same, albeit in its own language of information, fractals, holographic projections and very complicated mathematics! (The next book in this Wisdom series will go into much more detail about the new science, but hopefully in an intelligible way for the non-scientist!) The message is that there is an inherent oneness and unity to the whole of the universe, which seems to emanate from one source. Going back to some of the earliest religious writers, we have the Hindu Upanishads, dating from various stages of the first millennia BCE:

In the beginning was only Being; One without a second. Out of himself he brought forth the cosmos and entered into everything in it. There is nothing that does not come from him. Of everything he is the inmost Self. (Chandogya Upanishad, 6.2:2–3)

God is one, hidden in all beings, all-pervading, the Self within all selves, watching over all doing, dwelling in all being, the witness, the perceiver, the single one, free from all qualities. (Svetasvatara Upanishad 6:11)

The Buddha had his experience of enlightenment, which led to a new perception of life:

He who experiences the unity of life sees his own Self in all beings. (Gautama Buddha, d. 544 BCE)

In China, around the same time, was LaoTzu:

Can you dissolve your ego? Can you abandon the idea of self and other? Can you relinquish the notions of male and female, short and long, life and death? Can you let go of all these dualities and embrace the Tao without skepticism or panic? If so, you can reach the heart of the Integral Oneness. (Laotzu, sixth century BCE)

Slightly later in India came the Bhagavad Gita, where Krishna says,

The whole world is pervaded by Me, yet my form is not seen. All things have their being in Me, yet I am not limited by them. (Bhagavad Gita 9:17–19 (circa fourth to second century BCE))

The Hebrew Scriptures contain the story of Moses and the burning bush, out of which the voice of God spoke to him. Moses was instructed to go back to Egypt, to rescue the Israelites, and he asked who was this that was sending him:

God said to Moses, "I AM WHO I AM." He said further, "Thus you shall say to the Israelites, 'I AM has sent me to you.'" (Exodus 3:14)

The Hasidic Hebrew understanding of the text is that God is all that is. God is all that is happening at every moment. God is I AM – not a being or even a supreme being, but *Beingness* itself. The prophet Isaiah said as much:

I am the One Who Is, there is nothing else. (Isaiah 45:5)

In the early Christian era, we find Jesus saying almost the same. Complete oneness is the aim:

May they be one, as we are one, I in them and you in me, that they may become completely one. (John 17:22–23)

In the suppressed Gospel of Thomas, from the Nag Hammadi texts – now thought to contain some of the earliest sayings, predating Paul's letters – we find the idea that the Christ is omnipresent:

Jesus says: I am the light that is over all things. I am all: from me all came forth, and to me all attained. Split a piece of wood; I am there. Lift up the stone, and you will find me there. (Gospel of Thomas saying 77)

And St Paul himself affirmed that everything is in God when he said:

In God we live and move and have our being. (Acts 17:28)

Christianity asserts that God is Beingness, and we have our individual being within that One Being, which came to be seen as the Cosmic Universal Christ.

In the second century, Marcus Aurelius was Roman emperor from 161 to 180. He was the last of the rulers traditionally known as the Five Good Emperors and has been called "the Philosopher". He made this rather remarkable statement:

All things are linked with one another, and this oneness is sacred; there is nothing that is not interconnected with everything else. For things are interdependent, and they combine to form this universal order. (Marcus Aurelius 121–180 CE)

These are remarkable insights from one thousand nine hundred years ago, which could have been written yesterday. The universal order is that everything is interconnected in the sacredness. It is mystical understanding. Later, we reach the Christian mystics, who had the same level of insight. Hildegard of Bingen lived from 1098–1179 CE and was a German Benedictine abbess, a writer, composer, philosopher, mystic, visionary, healer and polymath. Quite a woman!

> *I (God) am life itself. For I am the whole of life – life was not torn from stones; it did not bud from branches; nor is it rooted in the generative power of the male. Rather, every living thing is rooted in me... I am the life that remains the same through eternity.*
> (Hildegard of Bingen, in Nash, 1997, p.19)

> *Everything that is in the heavens, on earth, and under the earth is penetrated with connectedness, penetrated with relatedness.*
> (Hildegard of Bingen)

A little later, there was Eckhart von Hochheim (c. 1260–c. 1328), commonly known as Meister Eckhart. He was a German theologian, philosopher and mystic. In later life, he was accused of heresy and brought before the local Dominican-led Inquisition, to be tried as a heretic by Pope John XXII. He seems to have died before his verdict was received, fortunately for him, as being judged a heretic could involve much suffering.

> *Dare to dwell in that single oneness beyond every hope of gain, where nothing separates you from God.*
> *What is Love? To realise that God is one and I am one in this One.*
> *This, I tell you, is true: in eternity, everything is present at*

once, and everything is one.
(Meister Eckhart in Burrows & Sweeney, 2019, pp. 54, 87, 99)

Around the same time, this statement from John van Ruysbroeck, a Flemish mystic, is virtually saying the universe is holographic:

The image of God is found essentially and personally in all. Each of us possesses it whole, entire and undivided, and all of us together do not possess it more than one person does alone. In this way we are all one, intimately united in our eternal image, which is the image of God. (John van Ruysbroeck, 1293–1381 CE)

It gives a whole new meaning to the verse in Genesis that says: "So God created humankind in his image, ... male and female he created them" (Genesis 1:27). If we are a holographic image of God, then we are a projection, an emanation of the cosmic mind. In holographic images, any individual piece if broken off, no matter how small it is, still contains the whole image. Van Ruysbroeck is saying the same – we somehow share in that unity which we call God, as does the whole of creation. A little later, in Ukraine, Rabbi Heller (ca. 1742–1794) from the Jewish mystical tradition made the same emphasis that everything is God:

There is nothing in the world other than God and God's emanated powers which are a unity. Other than that, nothing exists. Although it seems that there are other things, everything is really God and the divine emanations. (Rabbi Heller of Zbarazh)

Then we reach more contemporary writers. William James we have already heard from at the beginning of this chapter, saying that: "In mystic states we both become one with the Absolute and we become aware of our oneness." Just a little later, the great scientist Albert Einstein wrote a private letter to a grieving friend, saying:

A human being is a part of a whole, called by us "universe", a part limited in time and space. He experiences himself, his thoughts and feelings as something separated from the rest... a kind of optical delusion of his consciousness. This delusion is a kind of prison for us, restricting us to our personal desires and to affection for a few persons nearest to us. Our task must be to free ourselves from this prison by widening our circle of compassion to embrace all living creatures and the whole of nature in its beauty. (Albert Einstein, 1879–1955)

Father Bede Griffiths (1906–1993), the Benedictine priest who went to India and became known for integrating Christianity with Hindu thought, made the distinction between individual and universal consciousness:

There is no doubt that the individual loses all sense of separation from the One and experiences a total unity, but that does not mean that the individual no longer exists. Just as every element in nature is a unique reflection of the one Reality, so every human being is a unique centre of consciousness in the universal consciousness.... All our seeing, and hearing and perceiving and knowing, is an effect of and a participation in the consciousness of that one, universal Being. (Griffiths, 1982, p. 90)

This idea of the one universal being, the One Reality is across all main religious beliefs. Bede Griffiths was an inspiration for John Main, founder of the World Community for Christian Meditation. Main's writings were full of references to oneness, unity, fullness, wholeness and similar concepts.

The way of simplicity is the way of the one word, the recitation of the one word. It is the recitation, and the faithfulness to that recitation every morning and every evening, that leads us beyond all the din of words, beyond all the labyrinth of ideas, to oneness....

Meditation is a way into full communion, oneness of being.... Not only do we discover our own oneness, but we discover our oneness with the All and with all. (John Main, 1989, p. 19)

Meditation is the way to a fulfilled state of being.... All sane action in our lives must flow out of being at one with being. This means that to meditate, we begin to learn to be wholly alert; to accept oneself wholly; to love oneself; and to know oneself rooted and founded in the utter reality that we call God. (John Main, 1989, p. 117)

This is what the practice of meditation is truly about, being rooted in the oneness of God. This oneness is not just about humanity, it is about everything on this planet. It is all-embracing. Science tells us that we are essentially vibratory patterns, interacting, communicating informational energies. We are slowly evolving into an awareness that oneness and compassion is the way ahead. The mystics and seers and pioneers have always been dancers on the edge with this idea, dancing on the edge of orthodoxy, trying to stay within its bounds – otherwise in the past they could be condemned as heretics and outcast, at worst burnt at the stake, decapitated or even hung, drawn and quartered. They are on the edge because they have seen something which is hard to put into words, but which they know – it is seared into their hearts and minds – that we are one with the Divine essence which permeates and holds everything! What separates us is that we are bound up in our own personalities, our bodies, our emotions and our thoughts. This is the prison of our egoic self-experience. Our egos, attitudes, opinions, beliefs, fears, hang-ups, and general human nature keep us tied down to this level of reality. But at a deeper, fuller, more whole, soul level, we are one with the All, with the Universal Christ Energy as expressed in the Christian tradition.

The mystics and seers couched their deep writings in

acceptable terms for the times they lived in. From a religious perspective, people call this Divine one essence by different terms in different belief systems – God, Allah, Brahman, the One Life, the Source, the Absolute Ultimate Reality. The scientists are now beginning to call it the cosmic Information Field, or just "Mind". The new perception is, we are all one in the divine presence that sustains us all. Jesus demonstrated this for us as the union of human and divine within space and time here on this planet, and the Universal Christ is the eternal union of matter and Spirit from the beginning of time, into which we can begin to reach with our perception through mystical experiences of Oneness with the Divine nature.

Questions for Reflection

1. What questions do you have about this concept of the Universal Christ? Try writing them down to make your thoughts clearer.
2. Have you ever had what you would term a mystical experience? What effect did it have on you?
3. How has your experience of Christian liturgy and hymns shaped your understanding of Jesus the Christ?

A Contemplative Practice
Centering Prayer

Thomas Keating was one of the founders of Centering Prayer, a Christian contemplative practice based in early desert monasticism, texts like *The Cloud of Unknowing*, and mystics Teresa of Ávila (1515–1582) and John of the Cross (1542–1591). Centering Prayer is a practice in letting go of thoughts, one after the other after the other. It retrains the brain into an open, yielding awareness. Each passing thought is seen simply as an opportunity to return to God, to awareness of the Divine Presence, using the sacred word as an anchor for the mind. It is one form of meditation, the foundational practice for entering into mystical experience.

Here is the simple method for Centering Prayer as taught by Keating. His teaching was to do this for twenty minutes every day. When used over many years, it bears fruit as our consciousness moves to a more compassionate and loving level of being.

- Choose a sacred word as the symbol of your intention to consent to the Divine presence and action within.
- Sitting comfortably and with eyes closed, settle briefly and silently introduce the sacred word as the symbol of your consent to the Divine presence and action within, repeating it slowly.
- When engaged with your thoughts [including body sensations, feelings, images, and reflections], return ever so gently to the sacred word.
- At the end of the prayer period, remain in silence with eyes closed for a couple of minutes.

For more information on Centering Prayer, see www.contemplativeoutreach.org

Further Resources

Fox, Matthew, 1988. *The Coming of the Cosmic Christ*. New York: HarperOne

Johnston, William, 1995. *Mystical Theology: The Science of Love*. London: HarperCollins

MacGregor, Don, 2012. *Blue Sky God: The Evolution of Science and Christianity*. Alresford UK: Circle Books, John Hunt Publishing (especially Chapter 5 Rethinking Jesus)

Main, John, 1989. *The Way of Unknowing*. London: Darton, Longman & Todd

Underhill, Evelyn, 1911. *Mysticism*. London: Methuen & Co.

Chapter Six

The Christ and Other Faiths

Wisdom and Christ

I remember, in my evangelical fundamental days, being puzzled by reading about Wisdom in the Book of Proverbs chapter eight, which presents Wisdom as female (*Sophia* in Greek), and as the firstborn of God's creation.

> *The LORD created me at the beginning of his work, the first of his acts of long ago. Ages ago I was set up, at the first, before the beginning of the earth... When he marked out the foundations of the earth, then I was beside him, like a master worker; and I was daily his delight, rejoicing before him always, rejoicing in his inhabited world and delighting in the human race.* (Proverbs 8:22–23, 29–31)

Wisdom is described here like God's masterplan for creation and the first of his begotten creatures. This conflicted with my understanding of Christ at that time, which was (a) that he was male, and (b) that he was said to be the firstborn, according to Colossians:

> *He is the image of the invisible God, the firstborn of all creation.* (Colossians 1:15)

Could the female Wisdom be the male Christ, I wondered? So I looked further into this, turning to two books in the Apocrypha (that collection of texts that are included in the canon of Roman Catholic and Orthodox Bibles, but not Protestant ones).

> *There is in her [Wisdom] a spirit that is intelligent, holy, unique,*

manifold, subtle, mobile, clear, unpolluted, distinct, invulnerable, loving the good, keen, irresistible, beneficent, humane, steadfast, sure, free from anxiety, all-powerful, overseeing all, and penetrating through all spirits that are intelligent, pure, and altogether subtle... For **she is a breath of the power of God,** *and a pure emanation of the glory of the Almighty... For she is a reflection of eternal light, a spotless mirror of the working of God, and an image of his goodness. Although she is but one, she can do all things, and while remaining in herself, she renews all things;* **in every generation she passes into holy souls and makes them friends of God,** *and prophets.* (Wisdom 7:22–28)

I [Wisdom] came forth from the mouth of the Most High, *and covered the earth like a mist. I dwelt in the highest heavens, and my throne was in a pillar of cloud. Alone I compassed the vault of heaven and traversed the depths of the abyss.* (Sirach 24:3–5, also called Ecclesiasticus)

This Wisdom is very similar, maybe identical to the Christ of the New Testament, particularly in the words in bold above. The Prologue of John's Gospel starts "In the beginning was the Word" and the quote from Sirach above tells us the Wisdom came from the mouth of God, i.e., the Word, and is the breath and power of God. In addition, the use of the bread and wine in the gospels is foreshadowed by Wisdom crying out:

Come, eat of my bread and drink of the wine I have mixed. (Proverbs 9:5)

Come to me, you who desire me, and eat your fill of my fruits.... Those who eat of me will hunger for more, and those who drink of me will thirst for more. (Sirach 24:19,21)

St Paul actually calls Christ the Wisdom of God in 1 Corinthians 1:24. There is an obvious overlap between Wisdom and the

Holy Spirit as well, as *spirit* in both Hebrew and Greek can be translated as *breath,* and Wisdom is the *breath of the power of God.* As mentioned earlier, St Paul equates the Spirit of Christ with the Holy Spirit in Romans 8:9, so we have this interplay between Wisdom – Breath – Word – Spirit – Christ, which is all emanating from the one Source, called the Godhead in Christianity and the One Life in the Wisdom teachings.

Christ-Wisdom in Other Faiths

So it seems reasonable to equate the Wisdom of God with the Christ, this all-pervading Divine energy in the universe. This led me to thinking that Wisdom is not a term confined just to Christianity, as it is surely there in other faiths as well. I parked that one for many years as something to consider further at some stage! But when I became the Interfaith Officer for the Diocese, the question staring me in the face was: How is the Universal Christ/Wisdom Presence depicted in other faiths? Obviously, the term *Christ* would not be used as that is so specific to Christianity, so in what ways is this eternal, wise, abiding, loving, holding presence understood in other faiths? This series of books rests on the understanding that there is an underlying stream of Wisdom that is tapped into by all religions and particularly by those exalted humans who have been so inspired, and often deified, that they were the founders of a religion. Different faiths have their own interpretation of the Universal Wisdom Principle that we call the Christ in Christianity, and one way of looking for this is to discern the exalted beings of wisdom in the other faiths.

In Alice Bailey's writings, we find this principle clearly expressed:

We have seen that the doctrine of great Appearances and of the coming of Avatars or World Teachers or Saviours underlies all the world religions. Through Them, the continuity of revelation is implemented and humanity is enabled, each successive age, to take its next step forward along the Path of Evolution closer to God and that divine Centre in which the will of the One "in Whom we live and move and have our being" (as St. Paul expressed it in Acts XVII.28) is focussed, understood and directed... Some hard blow or some difficult presentation of the truth is badly needed if the Christian world is to be awakened, and if Christian people are to recognise their place within a worldwide divine revelation and see Christ as representing all the faiths and taking His rightful place as World Teacher. He is the World Teacher and not a Christian teacher. He Himself told us that He had other folds and to them He has meant as much as He has meant to the orthodox Christian. They may not call Him Christ, but they have their own name for Him and follow Him as truly and faithfully as their Western brethren. (Bailey, 1948, p.62–3)

Within the main world religions we have various terms which seem to apply to a cosmic person, an archetype. We have the Universal Christ-Wisdom within Christianity, and within other traditions we find similar concepts. The Cosmic Man, or Heavenly Man is an archetypical figure that appears in creation myths of a wide variety of cultures. This archetypal figure is seen coming into human incarnation, often as the one who has been sent to guide or save humanity. They are complicated concepts and there is not space to go into detail, but here is a brief outline.

Judaism: Within mystical Judaism and the teachings of the Kabbalah, there is the *Adam Kadmon*, the primordial man, as distinct from the earthly Adam, the first human being in the creation story in Genesis. Adam Kadmon is said to be the pure potential of divine light and, within the human psyche, the collective essence of soul. As mentioned earlier, the *Messiah* is a term that originated within Judaism, indicating the heavenly anointed human being who would save Israel from their current suffering. The term came to refer to a future Jewish king from the Davidic line, who will be "anointed" with holy anointing oil, to be king of God's kingdom, and rule the Jewish people during the Messianic Age.

In Zoroastrianism, which heavily influenced the Hebrew scriptures from the time of exile in Babylon, the *Saoshyant* or *Soshan* is an eschatological saviour figure who brings about the final renovation of the world in which evil is finally destroyed. The Saoshyant will prepare for them white *haoma*, the ritual drink of the Zoroastrians, which is said to bestow eternal perfection on their bodies.

Hinduism: In the earliest Hindu scripture, the Rig Veda, there is the figure of *Purusha*, the primordial cosmic Person in whom the whole of creation exists. Purusha is both immanent and transcendent and the whole creation comes forth from this cosmic person through the sacrifice of Purusha, which is reminiscent of the verse in the Revelation of John the "Lamb who was slain from the foundation of the world" (Revelation 13:8). Later, in the Upanishads, the idea emerges of Purusha as the great Lord of Light, who both transcends everything and yet is immanent in everything and dwells in the heart of each person.

> *He dwells in the heart of all, that Purusha not larger than the thumb dwelling within, always dwelling in the heart of each person. Each person is a person in that great Person.* (Svetesvara Upanishad 3:11.13)

The Purusha is within all, the universal Divine Person inhabiting all. Later still, in the Bhagavad Gita, thought to be written between the third and first centuries BCE, is the figure of Krishna, the cosmic Lord who says:

> *I am the One source of all. The evolution of all comes from me...*

In my mercy, I dwell in their hearts and I dispel their darkness of ignorance by the light of the lamp of wisdom... Know that with one single fraction of my being, I pervade the universe, and know that I AM. (Bhagavad Gita, 10: 8,11,42)

Krishna obviously bears a remarkable similarity to the Universal Christ figure, dwelling in the heart of all through Christ-consciousness, and even makes the same claim as Jesus the Christ did, "before Abraham was, I am" (John 8:58). There are many other similarities between the life of Krishna and of Jesus the Christ.

Buddhism: Within Buddhism, there is the concept of the *tathagata*, meaning the one who has "gone to that", the one who has realised the truth, and achieved complete enlightenment. A Buddha is a person who has manifested this truth and is the Absolute manifested in a human being. The teaching is that there have been many Buddhas prior to the current one, Gautama Buddha. A person who is on the path to buddhahood is called a *bodhisattva*, a path which stretches over aeons and many incarnations. Maitreya is regarded as the future Buddha of this world. According to Buddhist tradition, Maitreya is a bodhisattva who will appear on Earth in the future, achieve complete enlightenment, and teach the pure *dharma*, the ultimate truth. Maitreya Buddha will be the successor to the present Buddha, Gautama Buddha. (Within the Ageless wisdom teachings, Maitreya is the current holder of the position of Christ within the Hierarchy, but will, at some time in the future, move to hold the position of Buddha.)

Islam: Within Islam, no person can be associated with Allah, as that would be blasphemy. But within the Sufi teachings of the twelfth-century mystic Ibn al Arabi, the whole universe is conceived in terms of the oneness of being, the absolute reality called *al haqq*. The reflection of this oneness in the created world is that there is an archetype of the perfected Man, the mirror which reflects Allah. This perfect man is seen as the "idea" or "spirit of Mohammed". The perfected man is also seen in the *Mahdi* or *Imam Mahdi*, meaning the "Rightly Guided One". This is an eschatological Messianic person who, according to Islamic belief, will appear at the end of times to rid the world of evil and injustice. In Muslim traditions, it is said that he will appear alongside Jesus the prophet and establish the Divine kingdom of God.

The Universal Wisdom Presence

We begin to see the commonalities between many traditions, indicating that there is an underlying stream of thought and wisdom which emerges in different times and cultures and is thereby expressed in its own unique way within that tradition. This is what I would call the emergence of Universal Wisdom. Part of this is that there is an all-pervading universal presence that can fill a human being, enlightening and bringing to perfection, or to an exalted state, able to teach and impart wisdom to the masses of humanity. Matthew Fox, in his book *The Coming of the Cosmic Christ*, says,

> *Does the fact that the Christ became incarnate in Jesus exclude the Christ's becoming incarnate in others – Lao-tzu or Buddha or Moses or Sarah or Sojourner Truth or Gandhi or me or you? Just the opposite is the case... The Cosmic Christ needs to be born in all of us – no individual, race, religion, culture, or time is excluded. "Christ" is a generic name.* (Fox, 1988, p. 235)

Fox goes on to say that the term "Cosmic Christ" carries too much baggage, and that it can be replaced with "Cosmic Wisdom". As I pointed out earlier, the Bible texts indicate that we can virtually equate the Wisdom of God with the Christ, this all-pervading Divine energy in the universe. Fox gives a prophetic call from Cosmic Wisdom to the children of God to come together, saying,

> *Come, children, drink of my waters, which are all common waters.*
> *They are free and available to all my children. Let the Taoists drink*
> *and the Muslims drink; let the Jews drink and the Buddhists drink;*
> *let the Christians drink and let the native peoples drink. And then*
> *tell me: What have you drunk? How deeply have you imbibed my*
> *refreshment? What wet and running wisdom drips from inside you*
> *to the outside? What have you to share with others of my wisdom*
> *and harmonious living, of the dripping of oils of compassion?*
> (Fox, 1988, p. 244)

For me, the Perennial Wisdom teachings closest to Christianity are expressed in the writings of Alice A. Bailey, guided by the Tibetan teacher Djwhal Khul. Between them, they wrote twenty-four densely packed books between 1919 and 1949, setting out the coherent and complex cosmology of the Perennial Wisdom in great detail. One of the central tenets of this teaching is that there are seven streams or rays of divine energy that play out in the universe, and that our solar system is particularly influenced by the stream of Love-Wisdom, the Second Ray. This ray has a close association with the Christ principle, which is the Love-Wisdom-Consciousness stream within the three Divine aspects. Along with the other Rays, this stream of divine energy permeates and informs the gradual evolution of human consciousness, affecting all aspects of human society and slowly bringing human development to the next stage, a flowering of love and wisdom, leading to what Jesus termed the "kingdom of God".

Summary
The Hebrew Scriptures speak of Wisdom in the same terms as the New Testament speaks of the Christ, i.e., the Divine Word of God present from the beginning. This Wisdom emanates

from the Divine Source and can be found within the teachings of many other faiths. The Christ is the Love-Wisdom aspect of God as represented in Christianity, but it is not unique to Christianity. The idea of an archetype of a perfected human being who comes to redeem or purify humanity is also a theme within other faiths. It seems that a Universal Wisdom Presence is a common factor within all faiths.

I find the "well" analogy helpful: there are many wells that have been dug into the ground of faith, some deeper than others, but the well is only of any use if it reaches the water table and pure, refreshing water can be drawn from it. It is the same substance of water that is drawn from all the wells, the same sustaining, refreshing and essential ingredient for life. Once it comes up to the surface, it is then used in many different situations, contexts and cultures. But it is still the one water. All faiths, if they dig their well deep enough, reach that sustaining Wisdom at the bottom of the well. That is the Perennial Wisdom, which emerges in different times and contexts and was at the heart of the teachings of Jesus. He was a master wisdom teacher, giving out the teaching of inner transformation, that we are to love one another without self-centred egoic considerations, rising above our lower nature to bring in a new consciousness for humanity.

Questions for Reflection

1. Do you think the distinction between the Christ and Jesus can be introduced into institutional Church teaching? What form could it take?

2. Does an appreciation of the wise teachings of other faiths help with your own beliefs? If so, how?

3. Read about Wisdom in these passages: Proverbs 8, Wisdom 7:22–30, 9:9–18 and Sirach (Ecclesiasticus) 4:11–19, 6:18–37, 14:20–15:10, 24:1–12. What reflections do you have on Wisdom?

Further Resources

Bourgeault, C., 2008. *The Wisdom Jesus: Transforming Heart and Mind – a New Perspective on Christ and His Message.* Boston: Shambhala Publications Inc.

Fox, Matthew, 1988. *The Coming of the Cosmic Christ.* New York: HarperOne

Griffiths, Bede, 1989. *A New Vision of Reality: Western Science, Eastern Mysticism and Christian Faith.* Springfield IL: Templegate Publishers (Very helpful are chapters 6 & 7 on the Cosmic Person in Christianity and other faiths)

Wikipedia has two very helpful articles titled "Religious Perspectives on Jesus" and "Holy Wisdom"

Final Words

The New Testament is quite clear that the teaching of Jesus was to love one another, and it is reiterated throughout the Gospel of John and in many of the letters. (See John 13:34–5, 15:12, 17, Romans 12:10, 13:8, Ephesians 4:2, 1Thessalonians 3:12, 4:9, 2 Thessalonians 1:3, Hebrews 10:24, 1Peter 1:22. 3:8, 4:8, 1John 3:11,14,16,23, 4:7,11,12, 2John 1:5.) Within Christianity, this is taught as *agape,* or the unconditional love of God as seen in Jesus. But I believe it is a much bigger concept than this. Love is not just a sentiment or a feeling. The Wisdom teaching is that Love is the great principle of attraction, of desire, of magnetic pull, and (within our solar system) that principle demonstrates as the attraction and the interplay between materiality at all levels. This interplay provides every needed grade or type of unfoldment for consciousness. From the physical attractive forces within matter, bringing atoms into combinations of molecules and complex organic compounds, to the formation of cells and reproduction, to plant life, animal life and the establishment of the human form, it is all driven by Love, a Divine force and energy causing evolution and the growth of consciousness. It is all the love of God being manifested.

When the Christ came in the form of Jesus, he lived a life of love and service and gave humanity the new commandment, to love one another. This inaugurated a new age. After he appeared as the Avatar of Love, God became known as love (1John 4:8,16), to love one another became the goal (not just to love other Christians, but all humanity), love is seen as the basic principle of relationships, and love is working throughout all manifestation towards a plan motivated by love. This is the divine quality that the Christ revealed, and thus altered all human living and human goals. It has taken two thousand years for this truth to shape the form it has in the consciousness of the humanity today. Living as we do now in a global village, there is the realisation that our very future depends on us learning to live in relationships of loving understanding and goodwill towards each other, regardless of race, background, education and geographical location. This is the new fuel needed to keep the spiritual fire burning for humanity, as Tarkom Saraydarian writes:

Whenever a Teaching does not expand, it turns into dogma, doctrine, ritual and organizations; its spirit dies and the shell remains. The only way to keep the fire burning is to provide new spiritual fuel for it by having steady contact with the original Source of the Teaching. Great Teachers do not give the Teaching all at once. The Teaching is composed of a series of revelations which come one after the other in cycles, like the waves of the ocean.... They want us to receive the teaching, then live it and expand our consciousness in order to be able to receive the next revelation. But if we crystallize and accept the Teaching as formulas, words, dogmas, doctrines, and rituals, we will reject the new wave of the Teaching when it begins to hit our shores. No religion or Teaching can be final. It changes because of our growth and our expanding consciousness. (Saraydarian, 1990, p.64–5)

A new wave is coming, but change happens slowly. It is my belief that in order to survive in the twenty-first century as a credible belief, Christianity has to take on board some of the precepts and understandings of the Ageless Wisdom teachings, especially as the leading edge of science is now putting forward the idea that there is a universal consciousness from which everything stems at a deep level of reality. Human consciousness is evolving to finer, more compassionate vibrational levels of being, and many changes are happening in the world today that are beginning to reflect that. The dawning realisation that we are one interconnected whole, not just with the rest of humanity, but with all life in this biosphere, is a humbling truth that can unite us in mind and spirit. We look to a future in which harmony is a central aim of living, combined with compassionate hearts and altruistic minds for the good of all. This is the transformation at the heart of the teachings of Jesus the Christ.

Author Biography

Revd Don MacGregor, B.Sc. M.A., is a retired Anglican priest living in St Davids, Wales. He was a science teacher for 13 years before ordination, and his spiritual journey has moved from agnosticism to New Age to evangelical, charismatic Christianity, then deeper into mystical and esoteric teachings with an emphasis on meditation and contemplative prayer. He is passionate to find a new way forward for Christianity which incorporates twenty-first-century science and world-views. He is also an active member of the World Community for Christian Meditation, CANA (Christians Awakening to New Awareness) and the Progressive Christian Network.

Note to Reader
Thank you for purchasing *The Christ and Jesus: The Difference.* My sincere hope is that you derived as much from reading this book as I have in creating it. If you have a few moments, please feel free to add your review of the book at your favourite online site for feedback. Also, if you would like to connect with other books that I have coming in the near future, please visit my website for news on upcoming works, to sign up for new blog posts.

https://www.donmacgregor.co.uk

Don MacGregor, donmacg@live.co.uk

Previous titles
MacGregor, Don, 2020. *Christianity Expanding: Into Universal Spirituality. The Wisdom Series Book 1.* Alresford UK: **Christian Alternative Books, John Hunt Publishing**

Christianity Expanding – *Into Universal Spirituality* takes us on a whistle-stop tour of the areas that need updating if Christianity is to flourish in the twenty-first century. New science, ecological concern and the need for new theology are all converging into a maelstrom of change. With broad brushstrokes on a big canvas, a path of personal transformation is charted, drawing on the mysterious Perennial Wisdom teachings that have survived down the ages. Pulling no punches, Don MacGregor delves into typically taboo subjects such as reincarnation, drawing a distinction between Jesus and the Christ. This dynamic first volume of The Wisdom Series is an initial outline of areas that demand ongoing exploration.

Endorsements

Christianity is evolving rapidly today. Don MacGregor's book is a lucid and thoughtful guide to this process, and shows how the essential core teachings of Christianity can be disentangled from unhelpful interpretations that stand in the way of a living Christian faith in the twenty-first century.

Dr Rupert Sheldrake, author of *A New Science of Life* and *The Science Delusion*

With his deep and extensive understanding of Christianity and Perennial Wisdom teachings, Don MacGregor shares in this lucid, profound and wonderfully compassionate book that they, and indeed all major spiritual traditions, are the "path of the evolution of human consciousness".

Dr Jude Currivan, cosmologist, author of *The Cosmic Hologram* and co-founder of *WholeWorld-View*

MacGregor, Don, 2022. *Expanding Scriptures: Lost and Found. The Wisdom Series Book 2.* **Alresford UK: Christian Alternative Books, John Hunt Publishing**

In this second book in the Wisdom Series, Don MacGregor looks first at how we arrived at the existing text of the Bible. He then considers what could be added to the Bible from the intriguing rediscoveries of recent years and supports a new and central role for Mary Magdalene. Reinterpreting many texts and bringing out symbolic meanings, he also dives into the fascinating subject of numerology in the Bible and looks at how it can all be reframed within the Perennial Wisdom teachings.

Endorsements

Don MacGregor's little book, *Expanding Scriptures*, is a beauty. In a compact way, he covers an accurate history of the Bible, a wise and helpful understanding of biblical interpretation, a comprehensive look at "lost" gospels, and a well-researched understanding of the Bible for today's world. Highly recommended for personal study and group discussion.

Revd Paul Smith, co-founder of the Integral Christian Network, and author of *Integral Christianity: The Spirit's Call to Evolve*

Expanding Scriptures: Lost and Found is packed with direct, realistic spiritual wisdom, much needed for our modern world. Don MacGregor's words shine a bright light through the dark confusion of outdated thinking. This is cutting edge theology and a brilliant introduction to biblical history, including the lost gospels of the New Testament, the real Jesus and Mary Magdalene. Every Christian minister and Bible Study Group should read it. I promise the journey will be one of transformation and enlightenment.

Pam Evans MBE, Founder of the Peace Mala educational charity, and author of *How the Wisdom of the Ages Is Reflected in Many World Faiths*

MacGregor, Don, 2012. *Blue Sky God: The Evolution of Science and Christianity*. Alresford UK: Circle Books, John Hunt Publishing

Blue Sky God interprets some new scientific theories with blue sky thinking to bring radical insights into God, Jesus and humanity, drawing also on some deep wells from the past in the writings of the early Christians. In an accessible style, it looks at science research and theories in areas such as quantum physics and consciousness, epigenetics, morphic resonance and the zero-point field. From there, seeing God as the compassionate consciousness at the ground of being, it draws together strands to do with unitive consciousness and the Wisdom way of the heart. Throughout, it seeks to encourage an evolution in understanding of the Christian message by reinterpreting much of the theological language and meaning that has become "orthodoxy" in the West. In doing so, it challenges many of the standard assumptions of Western Christianity. It outlines a spiritual path that includes elements in all the world's great religions, is not exclusive, and yet has a place of centrality for Jesus the Christ as a Wisdom teacher of the path of transformative love.

Endorsements

This is a brave and important book, dispelling confusions and misunderstandings, and making clear the relevance of a Christian path today. MacGregor integrates modern science, mystical experience, history, philosophy and biblical scholarship in a new synthesis that shows how religious practice is evolving in the twenty-first century.

Dr. Rupert Sheldrake, author of *The Science Delusion* and *A New Science of Life*

This is a fascinating and profound exploration of the deep resonances between the discoveries of the Christian Mystics and those of modern science. We are living in an era in which mystical and scientific proof are coming ever closer to open up for the human race a wholly new way of approaching reality and potentially solving the enormous problems that keeping science and religion apart have created. I salute the courage of this book and hope it will attain a large and enthusiastic audience.

Andrew Harvey, author of *The Hope: A Guide to Sacred Activism, Son of Man* and others

Bibliography

Bailey, Alice A., 1937. *From Bethlehem to Calvary*. London: Lucis Press

Bailey, Alice A., 1948. *The Reappearance of the Christ*. London: Lucis Press

Borg, Marcus J., Wright N.T., 1999. *The Meaning of Jesus: Two Visions*. London SPCK

Blaiklock E.M. (trans.), 1983. *The Confessions of St Augustine*. London: Hodder & Stoughton

Borg, Marcus J., Wright N.T., 1999. *The Meaning of Jesus: Two Visions*. London SPCK

Borg, Marcus J., 2011. *Speaking Christian: Recovering the Lost Meaning of Christian Words*. London: SPCK

Bourgeault, C., 2008. *The Wisdom Jesus: Transforming Heart and Mind – a New Perspective on Christ and His Message*. Boston: Shambhala Publications Inc.

Burrows, M., Sweeney J., 2019. *Meister Eckhardt's Book of Secrets*. Charlottesville VA, Hampton Roads Publishing Co.

Comby, Jean, 1985. *How To Read Church History, Vol. 1*. London: SCM Press

Cranston, Sylvia, 1994. *Reincarnation: The Phoenix Fire Mystery*. Pasadena: The Theosophical University Press

De Mello, A., 1984. *The Song of the Bird*. New York: Doubleday.

Delia, Ilio, 2011. *Emergent Christ: Exploring the Meaning of Catholic in an Evolutionary Universe*. New York: Orbis Books

Eastcott, Michal J., 1966. *Jacob's Ladder: An Introductory Approach to the Ageless Wisdom*. Sedlescombe UK: Sundial House Publications

Fox, Matthew, 1988. *The Coming of the Cosmic Christ*. New York: HarperOne

Griffiths, Bede, 1982. *The Marriage of East and West*. London: Collins Sons & Co.

Griffiths, Bede, 1989. *A New Vision of Reality: Western Science, Eastern Mysticism and Christian Faith.* Springfield IL: Templegate Publishers

Hick, John, 1976. *Death and Eternal Life.* London: Collins, Fount.

Israel, Martin, 1992. *The Pain that Heals.* London: Arthur James

James, William, 1902. *The Varieties of Religious Experience.* London: Longmans, Green & Co

Johnston, William, 1995. *Mystical Theology: The Science of Love.* London: HarperCollins

King, Ursula, 2016. *Christ in All Things.* New York: Orbis Books

MacGregor, Don, 2012. *Blue Sky God: The Evolution of Science and Christianity.* Alresford UK: Circle Books, John Hunt Publishing

MacGregor, Don, 2020. *Christianity Expanding: Into Universal Spirituality.* Alresford UK: Christian Alternative Books, John Hunt Publishing

MacGregor, Geddes, 1989. *Reincarnation in Christianity.* Illinois: Quest Books

Main, John, 1989. *The Way of Unknowing.* London: Darton, Longman & Todd

Montefiore, Hugh. *The Christian Parapsychologist,* Vol 15, no.4, Dec 2002, pp.121–125

Nash, Wanda, 1997, *Gifts from Hildegard.* London: Darton, Longman and Todd

Nouwen, Henry J., 1990. *The Way of the Heart.* London: Daybreak, Darton, Longman and Todd

Rohr, Richard, 2019. *The Universal Christ.* London: SPCK

Rosen, Stephen, 1997. The *Reincarnation Controversy – Uncovering the Truth in the World Religions.* Badger CA: Torchlight Publishing

Saraydarian, Torkom, 1990. *The Ageless Wisdom.* Westhills CA: T.S.G. Publishing Foundation

Shapiro, Rami, 2013. *Perennial Wisdom for the Spiritually Independent: Sacred Teachings – Annotated and Explained.*

Woodstock VT: Skylight Paths Publishing.

Underhill, Evelyn, 1911. *Mysticism*. London: Methuen & Co.

Vermes, Geza, 2000. *The Changing Faces of Jesus*. New York: Viking Compass, Penguin Putnam Inc.

Weatherhead, Leslie, 1965. *The Christian Agnostic*. London: Hodder & Stoughton

THE NEW OPEN SPACES

Throughout the two thousand years of Christian tradition there
have been, and still are, groups and individuals that exist in
the margins and upon the edge of faith. But in Christianity's
contrapuntal history it has often been these outcasts and
pioneers that have forged contemporary orthodoxy out
of former radicalism as belief evolves to engage with and
encompass the ever-changing social and scientific realities. Real
faith lies not in the comfortable certainties of the Orthodox,
but somewhere in a half-glimpsed hinterland on the dirt track
to Emmaus, where the Death of God meets the Resurrection,
where the supernatural Christ meets the historical Jesus,
and where the revolution liberates both the oppressed and
the oppressors.

Welcome to Christian Alternative... a space at the edge where
the light shines through.
If you have enjoyed this book, why not tell other readers by
posting a review on your preferred book site.

Recent bestsellers from Christian Alternative are:

Bread Not Stones
The Autobiography of An Eventful Life
Una Kroll
The spiritual autobiography of a truly remarkable woman
and a history of the struggle for ordination in the Church of
England.
Paperback: 978-1-78279-804-0 ebook: 978-1-78279-805-7

The Quaker Way
A Rediscovery
Rex Ambler
Although fairly well known, Quakerism is not well understood.
The purpose of this book is to explain how Quakerism works as
a spiritual practice.
Paperback: 978-1-78099-657-8 ebook: 978-1-78099-658-5

Blue Sky God
The Evolution of Science and Christianity
Don MacGregor
Quantum consciousness, morphic fields and blue-sky
thinking about God and Jesus the Christ.
Paperback: 978-1-84694-937-1 ebook: 978-1-84694-938-8

Celtic Wheel of the Year
Tess Ward
An original and inspiring selection of prayers combining
Christian and Celtic Pagan traditions, and interweaving their
calendars into a single pattern of prayer for every morning
and night of the year.
Paperback: 978-1-90504-795-6

Christian Atheist
Belonging without Believing
Brian Mountford
Christian Atheists don't believe in God but miss him: especially
the transcendent beauty of his music, language, ethics, and
community.
Paperback: 978-1-84694-439-0 ebook: 978-1-84694-929-6

Compassion Or Apocalypse?
A Comprehensible Guide to the Thoughts of René Girard
James Warren
How René Girard changes the way we think about God and the
Bible, and its relevance for our apocalypse-threatened world.
Paperback: 978-1-78279-073-0 ebook: 978-1-78279-072-3

Diary Of A Gay Priest
The Tightrope Walker
Rev. Dr. Malcolm Johnson
Full of anecdotes and amusing stories, but the Church is still a
dangerous place for a gay priest.
Paperback: 978-1-78279-002-0 ebook: 978-1-78099-999-9

Do You Need God?
Exploring Different Paths to Spirituality Even For Atheists
Rory J.Q. Barnes
An unbiased guide to the building blocks of spiritual belief.
Paperback: 978-1-78279-380-9 ebook: 978-1-78279-379-3

Readers of ebooks can buy or view any of these bestsellers by clicking on the live link in the title. Most titles are published in paperback and as an ebook. Paperbacks are available in traditional bookshops. Both print and ebook formats are available online.

Find more titles and sign up to our readers' newsletter at http://www.johnhuntpublishing.com/christianity
Follow us on Facebook at
https://www.facebook.com/ChristianAlternative